Homemade Instruments

By Dallas Cline

Published originally under the title
Cornstalk Fiddle & Other Homemade Instruments

©Oak Publications
A Division of Embassy Music Corporation, 1976
33 West 60th Street, New York 10023

Music Sales Limited
78 Newman Street, W1 London

Music Sales (Pty) Limited
23 Clarendon Street, Artarmon, Sydney NSW, Australia

International Standard Book Number 0-8256-0186-X
Library of Congress Catalog Card Number 76-8073

Book and Cover Design by Carol Zimmerman
(Special thanks to Barbara Hoffman)

Cover and Interior Photographs by Herbert Wise
Drawings by Ellen Friedman-Weiss
Music Calligraphy by Ralph William Zeitlin

Contents

Introduction

It was a good many years ago that my mother showed me how to make a "banjo" from a kitchen matchbox and some elastic bands. For all the years following, I have found extreme delight in creating many kinds of melody and rhythm instruments, and in watching others find the same satisfaction in making instruments with their own hands. In numerous workshops with young children, we have turned out all kinds of strange-looking musical creations, some with strings, some percussion, but all of them able to produce tones and rhythms of one sort or another.

During the past years, with gatherings of music-making friends at home, we have conjured up all the sounds we could think of including the usual washtub bass, and the washboard with many tooting and thumping gadgets connected. I remember one night when a young man from Glens Falls came to a get-together with a gigantic instrument which he had concocted from the neck of a bass fiddle attached to the body of a great bass drum. He named this creation a "Clyde." It was a conversation piece, to say the least! Another group I knew used a typewriter for part of their rhythm section. Try it . . . it's tricky! And have you heard of the "rug-roll"? Can you imagine two people holding the ends of a rolled carpet, while a third one blows into the end through a tin-horn mouthpiece!

My mother and a favorite uncle both remember the cornstalk fiddles they made as children, taking the laces from their shoes to form the shoestring bow. There is an old song for this primitive little instrument:

> I got me a fiddle, and I got me a bow,
> And I learned to play the fiddle like Cotton Eye Joe.
> Cornstalk fiddle and a shoe-string bow,
> If that ain't a-fiddlin' then I don't know!

I've since made cornstalk fiddles with my own children. We've fashioned them from green August corn, which dries quite quickly, and they work beautifully with a little rosin on the shoestring bow. My husband John showed me how to make a willow whistle the way his grandfather taught him when he was small. I cannot ever forget sitting on a high wall overlooking the Hudson River, watching John use his penknife to loosen the bark on a small willow branch, to make the wood slide easily inside. How excited I was when the whistle came to life with strains of "Aunt Rhody"!

A few years ago, a friend and folksinger who had sat and listened to me carry on about one homemade instrument after another suggested I make a small book of instructions so other people could share in making them. This spurred me on to make more, and to ask others about simple instruments they knew of, or might have made themselves. I heard Margaret MacArthur playing a "bread board zither," found in an old barn in Vermont, and I made one for myself. Then I found that by changing the string arrangement on another board, I had a simple psaltry. So the collection of instruments grew, and the pages of the little book grew. It is like eating peanuts. . . . I just didn't quite know where to stop.

Now that I've stopped collecting and making, long enough to get it all down on paper, here it is. You can use this book at home on rainy days when there's "nothing to do"; a project which can easily develop into a family jugband. It can be used in schools to help young people become more involved in the music they are making. Perhaps it will suggest ideas for camp projects. Everyone, everywhere, can find something here for himself, and get started making his or her own music.

If anyone has any more ideas for instruments, easy to make or play, I would love to see, or hear about them. Once you become involved, you will find yourself trying to make instruments from everything you see! Would you believe . . . someone just called me about an old radiator!

—Dallas Cline

Before You Begin

To The Young People Who Use This Book

One of the most exciting, happy things we can do in life is to make music. Playing music with one other person, or in a group, is a joyful, sharing experience. Alone, music can be like a close friend, helping us to express our happiness, and sometimes helping us to get through very lonely, hurting times. It is a language which is as important to people as the languages we speak, and it is the only language which people all over the world share together. There is no problem in not knowing the right words!

If someone asked me to draw a picture of how music looked, I might draw it as a great tree. The roots would be the rhythm. The trunk and branches would be the melody, and the leaves and flowers would be the words to sing. Our feelings, which we put into the music we play and sing, could be like the wind and the rain that blows through the tree branches. The reason that the roots stand for rhythm is that we cannot have music without rhythm, as a tree cannot grow without roots. It is the most important thing to work on when you begin to make music!

Many of the instruments which you can make from this book are to use in making rhythms. Listen carefully to some music on the radio or on your phonograph, and practice keeping time to it. Use the different rhythms which are diagrammed for you, and try some of your own!

The melody instruments will help you in learning how to pick tunes out "by ear," or to make up your own melodies. And you can write words for your songs. It doesn't matter which comes first— just do it the way you feel it!

In making these instruments, you will learn a lot about sound and how it "works," such as the different sounds that come from rubber, wood and metal. You will learn these things, not because they are written down, but because you will try them for yourselves! Knowing all this helps you to understand the music you are playing even better! Do remember that some of these instruments are very primitive, and, like the cornstalk fiddle, will have only a little squeak. Some of the others will not tune up perfectly because you cannot possibly turn out fretboards with exact fretting, or chimes with exact pitch, unless you have much fancier equipment than we are using. Still, there is much fun to be had from all of them! You can play tunes and make lots of music!

In using this book, improvise if you need to! For instance, if a #5 screw is specified and you have a #4 or a #6, or even if you know only that the screw you have is small, go ahead and use it if it fits! If you don't know in what store to find something you need, use the telephone (the yellow pages can be a big help). You'll save your parents lots of running around. Hardware companies that stock plumbing supplies will often carry just the things that you need. I use dowels constantly, but good straight sticks or strips of wood are fine instead. Practice using any tools which are new to you before you start on a project. And remember to clean edges and surfaces of wood by sanding them before you glue (Elmer's white glue is excellent to use).

Be inventive and creative if you have ideas of your own. Try them out! Above all . . . have a joyful time, and make lots of rollicking good music!

How To Read Diagrams
For Rhythm And Melody

Using Letters for the Notes:

A̲ B̲ C̲: Underlined letters are low notes.

D E F G A B: Letters with no lines above or below are middle notes, and used most often.

C̄ D̄ Ē: Letters lined above are high notes.

Symbols for Keeping Time and Rhythm:

Lines drawn horizontally (＿) are equal to quarter notes and may be counted as 1 & 2 & 3 & 4 &.

Slash marks (/ /) are equal to eighth notes and may be counted as 1 & 2 & 3 & 4 &.
/ / / / / / / /

＿＿ = one whole count or 1 + or ♩

/ / = two half counts or 1 + or ♪♪

/ = one half count, either 1 or +

/ / = ＿＿ or ♪♪

o o = silent whole count, or 1

o = silent half count, either 1 or +

Dark lines show heavy beats, and light lines, light beats.

Examples:

One two three four   One two three

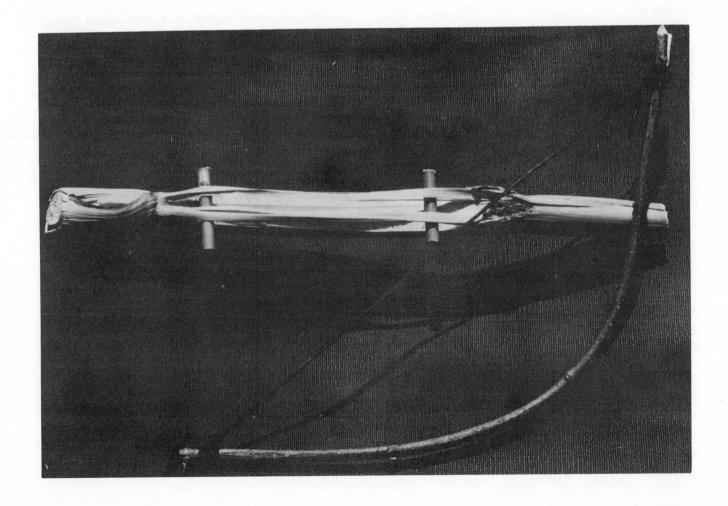

Rhythms For Drums And Rhythm Instruments

Now, you have all these marvelous drumsticks and rhythm instruments around, but somehow the drumbeats don't feel quite right, or sound like the ones on the radio. Let's try a few simple beats using just fingers first, and then you can use the same ones with drumsticks, maracas, or what-have-you.

We will use two basic patterns, one for 4/4 time that counts "one, two, three, four," and one for 3/4 time that counts "one, two, three." To make more interesting rhythms, you can add an "and" in between each of these numbers when you count. Then it looks like 1 & 2 & 3 & 4 &, or 1 & 2 & 3 &.

Hold the first two fingers of your right hand together and tap on the edge of your desk or table. Count out loud: one, two, three, four. Each time, rap the table. Now, do it twice as fast counting: one and, two and, three and, four and. Here's the way we'll make this look, so it's easy to read:

```
1 +  2 +  3 +  4 +     1 + 2 + 3 + 4 +
___  ___  ___  ___     / / / / / / / /
```

Now try two long beats and four short (half) beats, and go on with some variations:

```
1 +  2 +  3 + 4 + or: ___ ___  / / / /
___  ___  / / / /    ( ♩   ♩  ♫  ♫ )

1 +  2 +  3 + 4 +
___  ___  / / / /

1 +  2 +  3 +  4 +
___  ___  / /  ___
```

```
1 +  2 +  3 +  4 +
___  / /  ___  ___

1 +  2 +  3 + 4 +
/ /  / /  / /  ___
```

Here are some broken rhythms that are fun! They are all 4/4 time, and one has a silent beat:

```
1 +  2 +  3 +  4 +
___  /   ___  / /

1 +  2 +  3 +  4 +
___  / /  ___  o o
```

Here are some rhythms for 3/4 time. Count "one, two, three" for these, and sing songs like "Old Smokey," "Down In The Valley," or "Clementine."

```
1 +  2 +  3 + or: 1 + 2 + 3 +
___  ___  ___     / / / / / /
                  ( ♫  ♫  ♫ )

1 +  2 +  3 +
___  / /  / /

1 +  2 +  3 +
___  ___  / /

1 +  2 +  3 +
___  o o  / /
```

Keep time with your fingers while you sing, and after some practice, try the drumsticks or one of the other rhythm instruments.

Simple Toys

Stick Fiddle or Cornstalk Fiddle and Shoe-string Bow

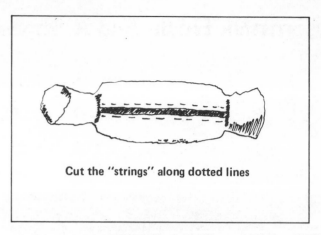

Cut the "strings" along dotted lines

Materials for the Stick Fiddle:

Stick or branch (not dead wood) about 15" long

Carpet thread, very fine wire, or music string (from a guitar or banjo or the like)

Two tiny nails

A small hammer

Two small sticks, each about 1" long

Tack the two nails into each end of the long stick, about 2" in from each end. Wind the thread or string around each nail, making it fairly tight, and close to the stick. Be sure it is secure at each end, so it won't pull off. Put the two small sticks under each end about an inch away from the nails. These will be your bridge and nut to hold the string up from the neck. Your stick fiddle is ready to play after you make a shoestring bow.

Materials for the Cornstalk Fiddle:

One cornstalk gathered in the middle or end of August, or when it has ripened and is almost ready for harvesting. (Find a farmer out in the country, and he will certainly be willing to give you one. You can even grow one in the back yard.)

Two small sticks, about 1" long each

Penknife or pocket knife

Cut the cornstalk above and below the two joints. The section between the two joints will have a groove running down one side. Take your penknife and cut very carefully under the highest edges on the sides of the groove. Cut from joint to joint, but not too close to either end. This will give you a "string" on each side. Keep these strings wide enough so they won't break. To raise the strings up from the fiddle, insert the two small pieces of stick crosswise under the strings, one at each end.

Materials for the Shoestring Bow:

Small thin twig or branch, about 14" long

Shoestring or shoelace

Penknife or pocket knife

Notch both ends of the small branch for the bow. Tie the shoestring or shoelace at each notch, putting a bend in the branch so it looks like a small bow-and-arrow set. The music which comes from one of these marvelous toys is a small, squeaky fiddle sound. To increase and improve the sound, you may use a little violin rosin, and rub it down the string. Rosin can be purchased at any music store. It works wonders, and the squeak will be really rewarding! It's a fine accompaniment for a song called "Cornstalk Fiddle and a Shoestring Bow." Run the bow back and forth across the strings, making a squeaky rhythm while you sing!

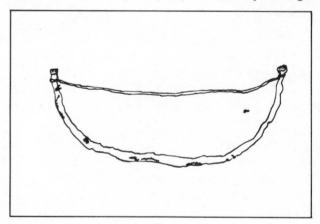

Cornstalk Fiddle And A Shoestring Bow

Traditional

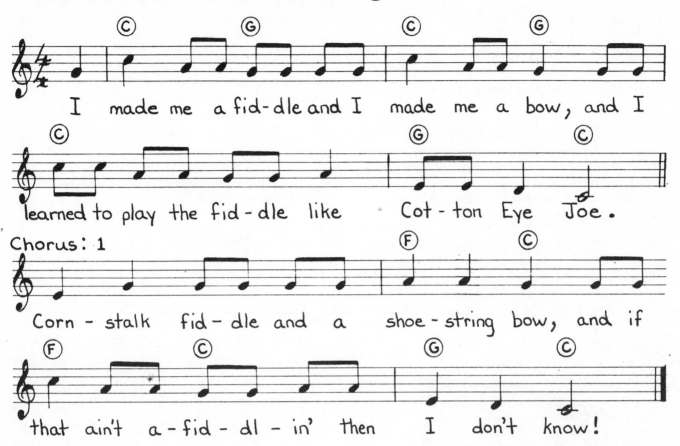

I made me a fid-dle and I made me a bow, and I learned to play the fid-dle like Cot-ton Eye Joe.

Chorus: 1

Corn - stalk fid - dle and a shoe - string bow, and if that ain't a - fid - dl - in' then I don't know!

Verse 1:

G C̄   A   A G   G   G   G C̄   A A G

I made me a fid - dle and I made me a bow,

G   G C̄   C̄ A   A G   G

And I learned to play the fid - dle

A   E   E   D   C̲

like Cot - ton Eye Joe.

Chorus 1:

E   G   G   G   G   G A   A   G

Corn - stalk fid - dle and a shoe - string bow,

G   G C̄   A   A G   G A   A   E D   C̲

And if that ain't a - fid - dl - in', then I don't know!

Verse 2:
I tuned up my fiddle and I went to a dance.
I tried to make some music but I didn't get a chance.

Chorus 2:
Cornstalk fiddle and a shoe-string bow,
It's the very best fiddle in the county-o!

Verse 3:
Cotton Eye Joe lived 'cross the creek.
He learned to play the fiddle
'bout seven days a week.

Chorus 1

Verse 4:
I've made lots of fiddles and made a lot of bows,
But I never learned to fiddle like Cotton Eye Joe!

Chorus 2

Matchbox Harp

Materials:

Large matchbox from wooden kitchen matches

Six rubber bands, of different sizes

One used wooden matchstick

Decorating the matchbox has two advantages. First, it makes the box stronger. Second, it takes longer to do the whole project and that makes it more fun! Be sure to let the paint dry carefully before you string it up.

Make six small notches in each end of the matchbox, one for each rubber band. Stretch the bands over the box and into the notches, and you're ready to play your harp. Pick the strings with the matchstick and make up some tunes for yourself. The different sizes of the rubber bands will make different tones. You can also use a small wooden box or frame which will be much stronger.

Shoebox Banjo

Materials:

Two medium-sized corks

Shoebox with lid

Large rubber bands

One 18" board (about 1" x 2") for the neck

Small scrap of wood about 1/2" high and 2" wide, for bridge, or use a small folded piece of cardboard, with four notches cut in the folded edge.

Tools and Hardware:

Glue

Scissors

A hammer

Two small nails

Cut a hole in the center of the cardboard lid. Cut a hole the size of the 1" x 2" stick for the neck at the edge of the lid, on one end. Cut another the same size at one end of the box. Put glue on one end of the stick and set in into the lid, with the end almost up to the sound hole. Let the lid and the stick neck sit with a weight on them for at least a half hour, until the glue dries.

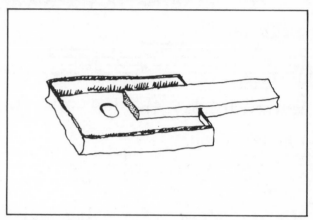

Cut holes for the corks just past the sound hole opposite the neck. Cut the holes just a little bigger than the small end of the cork. Push the corks halfway into the holes. At the other end, hammer the two nails about halfway into the neck, about an inch from the end. Put the lid and neck on the banjo box body, and add the elastic bands. String them around the corks and the nails. Put the wood strip or cardboard under the strings down near the sound hole. This is the "bridge" and holds the strings off the face of the instrument. Now is the time to STRUM AWAY!

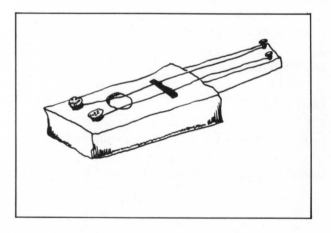

Willow Whistle

Materials:

A small branch about 1/2" in diameter, and about 8" or 10" long. You may use almost any smooth-barked wood, except maple, oak or hickory. Willow and ash seem to be the best. The selection of the right piece is most important and care should be taken that it be free of flaws.

Penknife or pocket knife

Cut one end off (A) evenly and cut through the *bark only* at the other end (B).

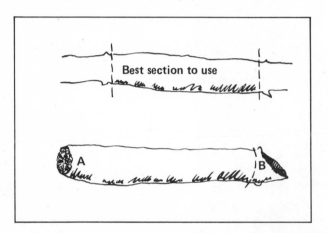

Rub the bark gently and evenly with the side of the knife handle. Do not press too hard or the bark may split.

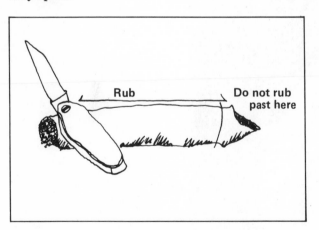

After rubbing section A, try to twist the bark loose. How hard to twist will come with practice. If it seems too tight, rub some more.

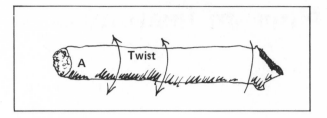

When the bark is loose, cut a notch in section A about 1" from the end.

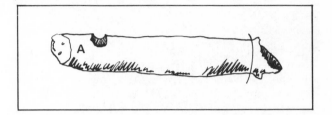

Now remove the bark from section A and cut the wood in two, at the notch.

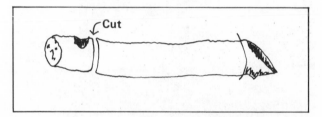

Cut away the shaded areas on the small piece.

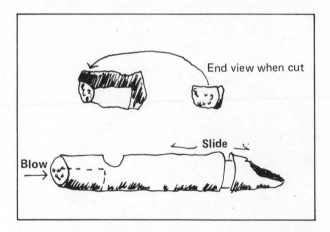

Place the small piece back into the bark, with the flat surface up. The big piece goes in the other end. The long section slides back and forth to change the sound and to make the notes. Try playing "Aunt Rhody" or some very familiar tune!

Rhythm Instruments

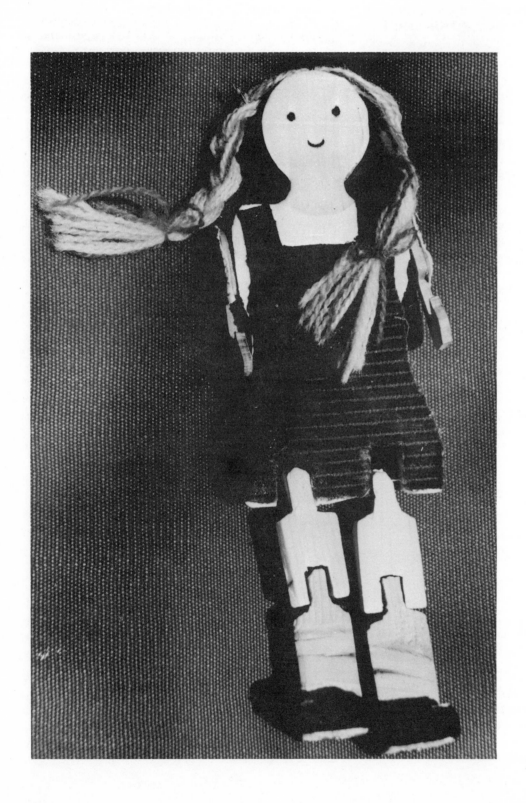

Clothespin Rattle Dolls

We used these dolls for dancing to music when were children, and had great fun decorating and dressing them with bits of fabric and paint and yarn. They may have painted hair, but it's better not to make yarn hair, which deadens the sound of the buttons. Pipe cleaners may also be used for arms to give them more dimension (glue a short piece to each side).

Materials:

One clothespin

Two 1" wooden or metal buttons with holes in the center.

A small hammer

A 1" long, very thin nail

Elastic band or thread

After the dolls are completely dressed and decorated, gently tack the buttons to the flat top of their heads, leaving enough room on the nail for a good rattling sound as you "walk" or "dance" them up and down across the table in time to the music. Tie the elastic to the top of the nail. Perhaps you could make a brother and sister, and attach them to opposite ends of a stick by tying the elastic to each end.

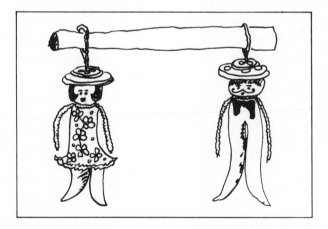

Dancing Spool Dolls

When we were children, our grandmother showed us how to make dancing dolls from empty thread spools. We used elastic bands, cut up and tied, for threading them; or sometimes heavy thread, which doesn't work so well. Now, we are fortunate, because elastic thread is available in all thicknesses.

Materials:

Ten medium-sized empty thread spools. (Two large spools, one a little larger than the other, looks even better for the head and body of the doll.)

Twelve buttons with four big holes in the center. (You could also use bottle caps, hammered flat with four nail holes.)

Elastic thread . . . very narrow size.

Lay out all the spools, so that the largest one is centered for the body, with two buttons between the body and the head. Put two buttons on top of the head.

Next, two arms go on each side of the neck buttons, with two buttons where the hands would be. Each arm has two spools. The legs go below, with two spools for each leg, and two buttons for each foot.

Run the elastic, knotted first, from the top of the head buttons down through the neck buttons and the body, on down through the leg spools and the foot buttons. Secure this by putting it through a second buttonhole, and go back up to the head again using different buttonholes. When all the way back up to the top of the head, tie the ends, leaving enough room for bounce!

Now thread another piece of elastic through the arms and arm buttons, running it under the neck buttons. Go all the way through and back again to tie them together, and cut the extra ends of the elastic off. Tie a string or elastic to the top of the head, and dance him in time to a song you sing, or something you play on the phonograph.

You may paint a face and clothes on your little dancer, which will give him lots of personality!

Bone Rattle

Materials:

Six or eight loin lamb chop bones . . . or any small round bones

One wire coat hanger

Ball of heavy twine

Tools and Hardware:

White glue

Wire cutters

To begin with, have lamb chops for dinner! Save the little round bones and wash them clean. Dry them in the sun for a few days.

Cut the coat hanger with the wire cutters, so that it's about 2 feet long. Bend it into a good, round circle, leaving about 4" on each end straight, for a handle. String the dried bones on this, and then twist the straight ends together once or twice. Put a dab of glue on one end of the twine, and start twisting it round and round the wire handle. When it has completely covered the wire, and looks like a comfortable handle, cut the twine, and dab it again with the glue to hold the end in place. Your bone rattle is complete, and you have a new sound to add to a rhythm section of your group—"Chop, chop, rattle and roll!"

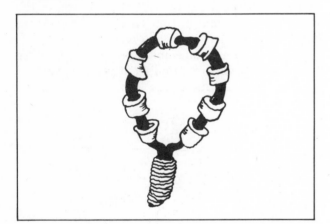

Finger Cymbals

Materials:

Four bottle caps for small cymbals

Four juice can lids for larger cymbals

Elastic, or rubber bands

A hammer

One medium-sized nail

Emery cloth

For bottle cap cymbals, flatten the caps by hammering them. Then hammer a nail hole into the center of each one. Smooth the hole down by tapping it with the hammer. With the juice can lids, do the same, putting a hole in the center of each one (use the emery cloth to smooth the sharp edges first).

Take all the flattened caps and lids, and one by one place them on a board which won't matter if it gets dented. Give each one a good WHACK, as close to the center as possible. Keep whacking until it makes a hollow around the nail hole. This helps it to have enough space between the two in a pair, so they have a good click when snapped together.

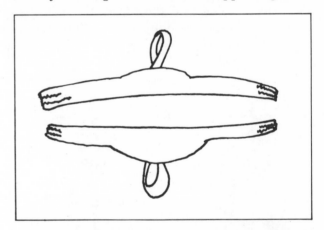

Put the elastic or rubber bands through each hole, and fit one end to your thumb, and the other to your middle finger. It should be comfortable, but not loose. Tie the remaining part in a very tight, small knot that won't slip through the hole. To play the finger cymbals, place them on the thumb and middle finger. Slap them together for rhythm. Make two pair and use them on both hands.

Try some of the rhythms on the rhythm page. (See the Table of Contents.)

The Gypsy Rover

The gyp-sy ro-ver come o-ver the hill, bound through the val-ley so

sha-dy. He whist-led and he sang 'til the green-woods rang, and

he won the heart of a la - - dy.

Chorus:

Ah-di-doh, ah-di-do-da-day. Ah-di-doh, ah-di-day-di. He

whist-led and he sang 'til the green-woods rang, and

he won the heart of a la - - dy.

		The	gyp-		
———	/	/		/	/
ro-	ver	come o-		ver	the
	/	/		/	/
hill,			Bound	thru	the
	/	/		/	/
val-	ley	so	sha-		
	/	/		/	/
dy.		He	whistled	and	he
	/	/		/	/
sang	'til	the	green-	woods	
	/	/		/	/
rang,		and	he	won	the
	/	/		/	/
heart	of	a	la-		
	/	/		/	/
a-			dy.		
	/	/		/	/

Chorus:

A-	di-		doh,	ah-	di-
	/	/		/	/
do-	da-		day.		
	/	/		/	/
Ah-	di-		doh,	ah-	di-
	/	/		/	/
day-			di.		He
	/	/		/	/
whistled	and	he	sang	'til	the
	/	/		/	/
green-	woods		rang,		and
	/	/		/	/
he	won	the	heart	of	a
	/	/		/	/
la-			a-		
	/	/		/	/
dy.					
	/	/			

Verse 2:

G G C D E - D C G G
She left her fa - ther's cas - tle gate,

G G C D E - F E D
She left her own true lo - ver.

G G C D E F G E C
She left her ser - vants, and her es - tate,

D E E E D C - A G C - A G
To go with the gyp-sy ro - o - ver.

Chorus:

G C D E D C G G
Ah - di - doh, ah - di - do - da - day.

G C D E F E D
Ah - di - do, ah - di - day - di,

G G G C C D
He whis - tled and he sang,

E F G E C
'til the green - woods rang,

D E E E D C A G C - A G
And he won the heart of a la - a - dy.

Verse 3:

Her father saddled his fastest steed,
Roamed the valley all over;
Sought his daughter at great speed,
And the whistling gypsy rover.

Chorus

Verse 4:

He came at last to a mansion fine,
Down by the river Clayde;
And there was music and there was wine,
For the gypsy and his lady.

Chorus

Verse 5:

"He's no gypsy, my father," said she,
"My lord of the freelands all over.
And I will stay 'til my dying day,
With the whistling gypsy rover."

Chorus

Sandpaper Blocks

Materials

Two blocks of pine board, or any wood about 3" x 4" x 1/2"

Two medium-sized bureau knobs, or two 3/4" pieces of 3/4" dowel

Tools and Hardware:

White glue or epoxy

Two pieces of medium-fine sandpaper 5" x 5"

Sixteen thumbtacks

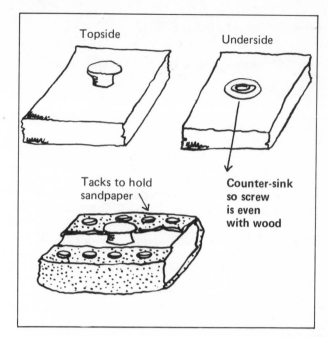

Topside

Underside

Tacks to hold sandpaper

Counter-sink so screw is even with wood

Sand the two blocks of wood until smooth (but not with the sandpaper you have for covering them!) Use the leftover ends when you cut the sandpaper to fit the block. There are two ways to attach either the bureau knobs or the dowel pieces for handles to the blocks. The first is easy, but not quite as secure as the second. First, you can simply glue the knob or dowel to the center of one side of the block. Clamp it, or weight it down with something heavy, for several hours.

The second way is to put the knob on as you would on a bureau drawer. Counter-sink the washer and head of the screw, on the side where the sandpaper will cover it. Then screw the knob down on the other side. To counter-sink something, you need a drill with a point the width of the washer, or a brace and bit. Drill in far enough to sink the washer and keep the head of the screw below the level where the sandpaper covers.

The last step is to cut the sandpaper to the exact width of the block, and then wrap the long edges over and around the sides to where the knob is. Pull as smooth and flat as possible. Then press the thumbtacks into the edges on both sides, to secure the paper.

To play the blocks, brush them gently back and forth against each other, keeping a steady rhythm. Try any of the rhythms from the rhythm page in the beginning of the book. When the sandpaper wears out, it is easily replaced.

Use the sandpaper blocks for rhythm while you sing "The Train Is A-coming." Make a rhythm which sounds like the train wheels turning: CHUG-a, chug-a, CHUG-a, chug-a. The triangle can accent the first beat each time, also.

Train Is A-Coming

Traditional

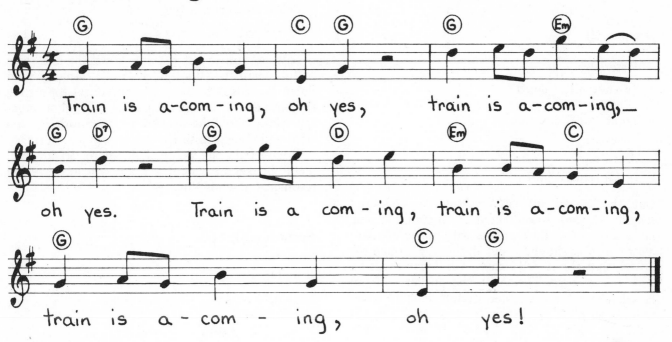

Verse 1:
Train is a - coming, oh yes,
/ / / / / / / / / / / / / / /

Train is a - coming, oh yes,
/ / / / / / / / / / / / / /

Train is a - coming, train is a - coming,
/ / / / / / / / / / / / / / / /

Train is a - coming, oh yes.
/ / / / / / / / / / / / / / /

Verse 2:
Engine is a - puffing, oh yes,
Engine is a - puffing, oh yes,
Engine is a - puffing, engine is a - puffing,
Engine is a - puffing, oh yes.

Verse 3:
Whistle is a - blowing, oh yes . . . (*etc.*)

Verse 4:
Johnny is the fireman, oh yes . . . (*etc.*)

Make up other verses using names for the conductor, engineer, brakeman, and ticket agent.

Scrapers

Scrapers (I)

Materials:

Two feet of 1/2" dowel

Tools and Hardware:

Sandpaper

Coping saw

Pocket knife or chisel

Cut the dowel in half, making two one-foot lengths. On one dowel, about 2" in from one end, cut a series of shallow grooves with the coping saw. These grooves should be cut all the way around the dowel, and about 1/8" apart. Go down about 5" with the grooves. Then with the pocket knife or chisel, dig out every other section, making wider grooves to play on. Leave the dowel smooth, but sand the ends of both. Finish off as you wish, using some type of hard floor finish or several coats of boiled linseed oil mixed with turpentine (equal parts of each). Hand rub in-between coats.

Play by rubbing the un-notched stick across the notches of the other in a favorite rhythm.

Scrapers (II)

Materials:

One-foot length of 3/4" dowel

Two- or three-foot length of 1/2" x 2" hardwood board

Tools and Hardware:

Coping saw or pocket knife

Sandpaper

Saw or whittle out notches down the 1/2" side of the board for about an 8" or 10" stretch. Sand down the edges to almost a roundness for sliding the scraper across easily. The 3/4" dowel or scraping stick should be sanded very smooth on the sides and ends. Finish the wood with a hard finish.

If you hold the notched board on an inverted metal bucket or a cookie tin it will improve the resonance. Buenos Notches!

Scrapers (III)

Materials:

Small wooden box (cigar box is fine . . . even a cardboard one)

One piece of striated plywood cut to fit the top of the box

White glue

Three of four thimbles to fit the thumb and two or three fingers

Glue the plywood to the top side of the box. (If it is a cigar box, cut the top off first.)

Don your thimbles and scrape away! Grate sound!

Use some of the suggested rhythms from the Rhythm section.

Tin Can Maracas

Maracas are a South American instrument, usually made of dried gourds, with handles on one end. They are shaken in time to the music. If gourds are not available, maracas can be made from tin cans.

Materials:

Two tin cans with plastic lids (orange juice or dog-food)

Two 8" to 10" dowels, 1/2" diameter. The length depends on the size of the cans you use. They need a good-sized handle.

Small stones or pebbles

Tools and Hardware:

Screwdriver

Plastic tape

Two wood screws with washers to fit into the ends of the dowels

Paint, if you are going to decorate the cans

Fill each can one quarter full of the small stones. (Beans will also work.) Tape the plastic lid down around the edge of the can. Puncture the metal bottom of the can with the screwdriver or a sharp punch in a small cross shape, so you can wedge the dowel into it. The dowel must be long enough to reach the other end of the can, and leave a comfortable handle to hold. Screw the small screw over the washer and into the plastic lid, and onto the dowel. This will steady the whole contraption.

Now you have one maraca, but you need a pair, so get busy and make the second.

You may paint and decorate them in bright colors and designs.

To play the maracas, use the left hand for the heavy beat, and the right hand for the off beats.

For example,

Left hand: Shake and   Shake and
Right hand: shake shake   shake shake

Left Hand: ___ o o ___ o o
             1 + 2 + 3 + 4 +

Right Hand: o o   / /   o o   / /

Also:

Left Hand: ___ o ___ o o o
             1 + 2 + 3 + 4 +

Right Hand: o o   / o o /   / /

Shake and . . . shake . . .

Aiken Drumm

Traditional

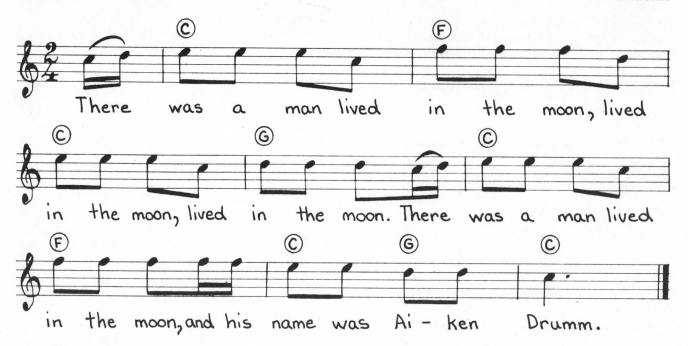

Verse 1:

___	/	___	/	/	/	There
was	a	man		lived		
/		/		/	/	
in	the	moon,		lived		
/		/		/	/	
in	the	moon,		lived		
/		/		/	/	
in	the	moon,		There		
/		/		/	/	
was	a	man		lived		
/		/		/	/	
in	the	moon		and his		
/		/		/	/	
name	was	Ai -		ken		
/		/		/	/	
Drumm.	___		/	/	/	

Chorus:

___	/	___	/	/	/	And he
played	up -	on		a		
/		/		/	/	
la-		dle,		a		
/		/		/	/	
la-		dle		a		
/		/		/	/	
la-		dle.		He		
/		/		/	/	
played	up-	on		a		
/		/		/	/	
la-		dle,		and his		
/		/		/	/	
name	was	Ai -		ken		
/		/		/	/	
Drumm.	___		/	/	/	

Verse 2:

C D E E E C F F
And his head was filled with cream cheese,

D E E E C D D
With cream cheese, with cream cheese.

C-DE E E C F F
His head was filled with cream cheese,

F F E E D D C
And his name was Ai - ken Drumm.

Chorus

Verse 3:
And his coat was made of good roast beef,
Good roast beef, good roast beef.
His coat was made of good roast beef,
and his name was Aiken Drumm.

Chorus

Verse 4:
And his hair was made of noodles,
Of noodles, of noodles,
His hair was made of noodles,
and his name was Aiken Drumm.

Chorus

　　Make up more verses for his nose, his eyes, his hands, and his feet, until Aiken Drumm becomes a full picture!

Coffee Can Bongos

Real bongo drums can be quite expensive, but coffee can bongos are a fun way to have yourself a set quickly and inexpensively for your next musical get-together!

Materials:

Two coffee cans with plastic tops. One can should be larger than the other.

Tools and Hardware:

Can opener

Two wing nuts and two bolts

A hammer

A large nail to make holes in the cans

First cut the tops and bottoms out of both cans. (Catch your mother just after her coffee klatch!) Then hammer the holes in the sides, bracing the inside so the cans will hold their shape while you work. The two holes in each can should be about three inches apart, in a straight line from top to bottom. The top hole in the taller can should be near the center, so it can be matched up with the top hole in the smaller can. The bottom rims of both cans should be even. Match up the two lower holes in both cans, and then put the wing nuts through them. Tighten the wing nuts and bolts very securely.

If you want to decorate them, do it before the heads are put on. For the drumheads, you may use the plastic lids, or you can be fancy and buy two small drumheads from the music store. With this you will need lacing also, and eight or nine small S-hooks.

Cut the drumheads about one inch larger than the drum all around the top of each can. Punch evenly spaced holes with a paper punch—four around the top for the smaller can, and five on the larger one. Put the holes in at least 1/2" from the edge. Soak the drumheads for about half an hour in lukewarm water, then lace them onto each can, hooking them into the S-hooks which are hooked onto the lower edges of the cans. Do not pull them tight. They will tighten as they dry.

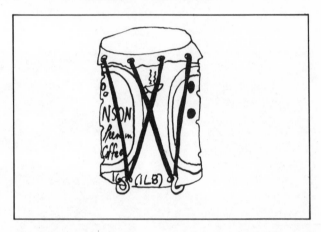

Let the heads dry overnight before you touch them. Now you are ready to beat out hand rhythms while you hold the bongos between your knees, one can against each knee. See the section on drum rhythms if you don't have some simple ones of your own. Practice with the radio; it's more fun!

Triangle

You have a choice of making an easy triangle from metal tubing, which bends with no effort, or a solid one which sounds louder, but is difficult to bend. You will probably need a vise for the solid one, and if you don't have a vise, try to find a friendly neighbor who has one you can use.

Materials:

Aluminum tubing, 19" long (old T.V. antenna or ask your local junk dealer)

3/8"-wide cold rolled steel rod, 19" long (from the hardware store)

A foot of cord or rawhide made into a loop

Tools and Hardware:

Hacksaw

Pliers

Steel file

Fine steel wool

File down both ends of the rod or tubing until smooth, tapering them to long points. The finer the taper, the higher the pitch of the finished triangle. Polish the entire thing with steel wool.

For either rod, measure 6" from each end, and bend into the shape of a triangle.

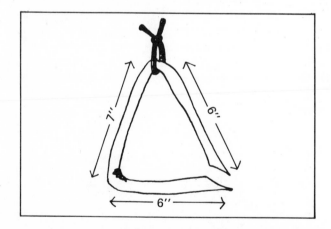

Make a striker from a pencil or dowel about 8" long. Tie the cord or rawhide loop at the top bend of the triangle to hold it. Now! You are ready to take the striker in hand and wait your turn in the rhythm band for that dramatic moment, when all is quiet, and you make three tingling beats on your triangle!

Tone Block or Clack Box

Materials:

Soft pine board 2" x 4" and about 6" long

Hardwood or wall paneling 1/8" thickness, 4" x 6" piece

Tools and Hardware:

Sharp chisel

Fine saw to cut 1/8" wood

Sandpaper

White glue

Mark off a line, across the wide side of the 2" x 4", about a 1/2" in from all four edges. Chisel into the wood from these marked edges until you have hollowed out the whole center section and reached about 1/4" thickness on the bottom. It may help to hold the wood in a bench vise while you are chiselling. (And be sure you have someone give you careful instructions if you have never used a chisel before. They are *dangerous* if not handled properly! Keep both hands in back of the chisel blade, and cut or push *away* from you.)

After the big portion is out in the main part, cut a section out of each end about 1/4" deep, to make an open space for sound when the top is on.

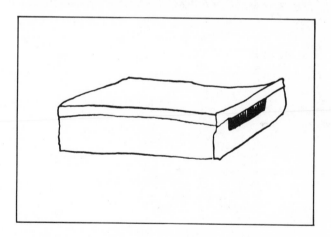

Put the top piece on and glue it all around. Let the glue dry under a good weight. (Again books or bricks are fine.) Sand the block to a smooth finish, and stain or varnish, as you wish. Sometimes several coats of good paste wax for floors makes a lovely satin finish.

Use a regular drumstick, or better yet, make your own! (See the Table of Contents.) This tone block is fun to use on the Devil's Dream!

I Was Born About Ten Thousand Years Ago

Traditional

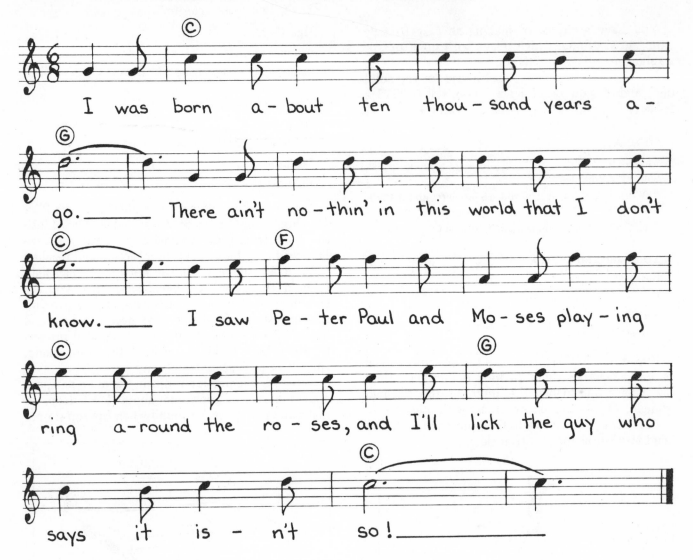

I was born a-bout ten
// / // / // /

thou-sand years a-go
// / / // // ///

There ain't no-thin' in this
/// // / // / // /

world that I don't know.
// / / // / /// ///

I saw Pe-ter, Paul and
/// // / // / // /

Mo-ses playing ring a-round the
/// / // / // // /

ro-ses, and I'll lick the guy who
// / // / // / // /

says it is-n't so!
// / // / / // /// ///

Verse 2:

G G C̄ C̄ C̄ C̄ C̄
I saw Sa - tan when he looked

C̄ B C̄ D G
the gar - den o' - er.

G G D̄ D̄ D̄ D̄ D̄ D̄
I saw Eve and A - dam dri - ven

C̄ D̄ Ē Ē
from the door.

D̄ Ē F̄ F̄ F̄ F̄ A A
From be - hind the bush - es peep - ing,

F̄ F̄ Ē Ē D̄ C̄ C̄
Seen the ap - ple they was eat - ing,

C̄ Ē D̄ D̄ D̄ D̄ B
And I'll swear that I'm the guy

B C̄ D̄ C̄ C̄
what ate the core!

Verse 3:
I taught Solomon his little A B C's,
Was the first one to eat limburger cheese.
And while sailing down the bay,
With Methusula one day,
I saved his flowing whiskers
  from the breeze.

Verse 4:
Queen Elizabeth fell dead in love with me.
We were married in Milwaukee secretly.
But I snuck around and shook her,
To go with General Hooker,
To fight mosquitoes down in Tennessee.

Make up a whopper of a verse yourself!

29

Dooley Stick

(so named and designed by Tony Johnson of Danbury, Connecticut)

Materials:

Bottle caps (gas stations or places selling bottled soda will give them to you, if you ask)

One pine board 2" x 2", about 5' long

Tools and Hardware:

Hammer

Three or four dozen #8 wire nails, 1 1/4" long

Get your friends together for a "Dooley Stick party," and you will be surprised how fast the bottle caps are ready for assembling.

Take out the cork or plastic insert from the inside of the bottle cap. Using the large nail, punch a hole in the center of the cap. Always punch from the outside to the inside. Take two bottle caps and, placing them back to back, put the smaller wire nails through the holes, and hammer them onto the stick. Do not nail them on tightly, as you want the caps to rattle freely against each other. Arrange them at least 1/4" apart on the stick.

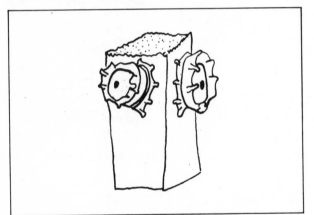

You may decide your own design or pattern for the caps on all four sides. You may want to put caps on three sides and decorate the other with the name of your group, or with attractive patterns. How about a plastic flower on the top?

To operate this instrument, you tap it gently on the floor, and it will make a tambourine-like sound, joined with the rhythmic tapping. It adds great color to any group or band.

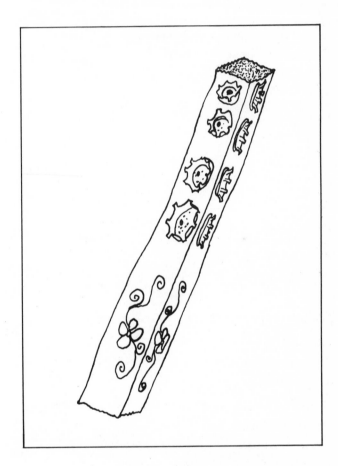

Pick A Bale Of Cotton

Traditional

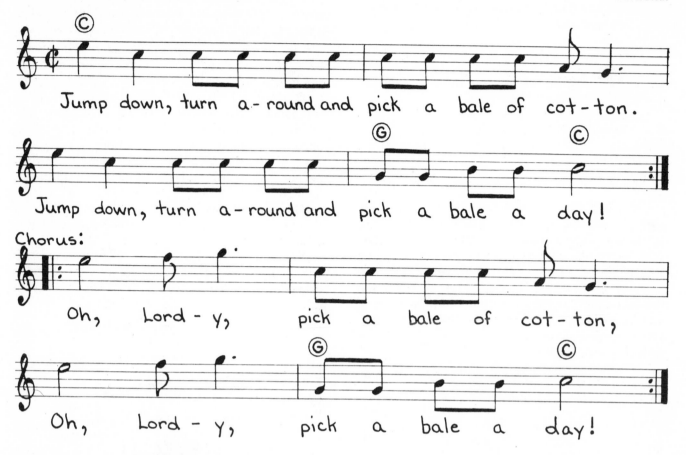

Tap the dooley stick where underlined:

Verse 1:
Jump down, turn a - round,
And pick a bale of cotton,
Jump down, turn a - round,
And pick a bale a day.

Jump down, turn around,
And pick a bale of cotton,
Jump down turn around,
And pick a bale a day.

Chorus:
Oh, Lordy, pick a bale of cot - ton.
(Shake dooley)
Oh, Lordy pick a bale a day!
(Shake dooley)

Oh, Lordy, pick a bale of cot - ton.
(Shake dooley)
Oh, Lordy, pick a bale a day!
(Shake dooley)

Verse 2:
E̅ C̅ C̅ C̅ C̅ C̅ C̅ C̅ C̅ A G
Me and my gal can pick a bale of cot - ton,
E̅ C̅ C̅ C̅ C̅ G G G B B C̅
Me and my gal can pick a bale a day. (Repeat)

Chorus:
E̅ F̅ G̅ C̅ C̅ C̅ C̅ A G
Oh, Lord - y, pick a bale of cot - ton,
E̅ F̅ G̅ G G B B C̅
Oh, Lord - y, pick a bale a day! (Repeat)

Verse 3:
Me and my wife can pick a bale of cotton,
Me and my wife can pick a bale a day. (Etc.)

Verse 4:
Went to Corsicana to pick a bale of cotton,
Went to Corsican to pick a bale a day. (Etc.)

Make up some verses of your own!

31

Cake Tin Hand Drum

Materials:

A round cake or candy tin, without the lid

Inner tube from a tire

Rawhide or heavy twine lacing

Tools and Hardware:

Scissors

Hammer

Paper punch

Can opener

Cut the bottom from the cake tin, and smooth down any rough edges by tapping it gently inside with the hammer. Cut open the inner tube so you have one flat length which will cover the two open sides of the cake tin. Lay the cake tin down and draw around it on the inner tube. Turn the tin over and make another circle connected to the first. Cut these two circles out like a figure eight, so they are connected together.

With the paper punch, make holes all around the edges, about every inch and a half. Pull this "drumhead" over the cake tin, so it meets on the side opposite the connected part. Tie this together to hold it in place until the lacing is complete. Now begin lacing with the rawhide or twine at one end near the connected side. Lace evenly all the way around until you reach the other end. Tie a good knot in the remaining twine, and cut it off leaving tails about an inch long. With more rawhide or twine, make a handle. You can make a braided handle, or use a single length of the twine and tie it into the lacing, making a loop large enough to hold in one hand.

The drumheads may be painted with very strong, bright colors in any kind of design you wish.

You will probably want to make a drumstick with a hard ball on one end, or use the wooden drumstick. Be free with your rhythm. . . . Try all kinds, and also try it while you sing!

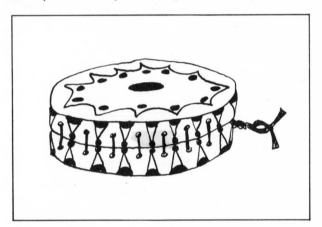

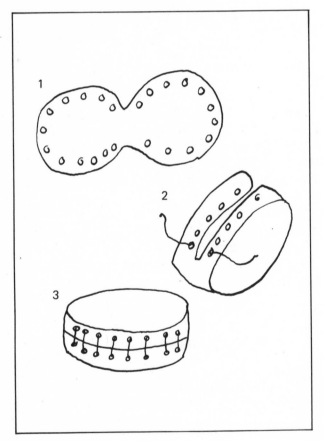

All Kinds of Drumsticks

Wooden Drumsticks

Materials:

12" to 14" lengths of 1/2" doweling

Penknife or pocket knife

Sandpaper

Make a mark about 5/8" from one end. With the penknife, cut a groove out around the dowel. Round off the small end, and make a slant toward the groove on the long end. Always carve away from yourself! When you are happy with the shape, sand it very smooth. If you like, you can put on several coats of paste wax (for floors) for a good finish.

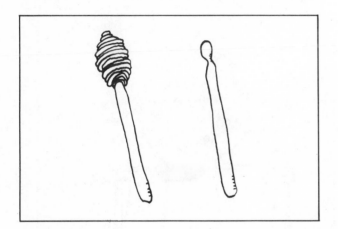

Other Easy Drumsticks

Wind yarn dabbed with glue around the end of any stick until it's the size you want it. Cut the end and hold it in place with the glue. Let it dry well before using.

Wooden beads, drilled out and glued on the end of a thin dowel or stick, make fine tom tom sticks.

How about a bouncy drumstick made from a small rubber ball? Cut a small hole in the ball to fit over a stick, and glue them together.

Even a pencil with a good rubber eraser on one end and unsharpened on the other, can be used on a small drum.

Last but not least . . . how about a "drumstick" drumstick? Chicken is pretty small, but a turkey drumstick might work well! Dry it in the sun before you try it. It's a good reason for having a turkey dinner, yes?

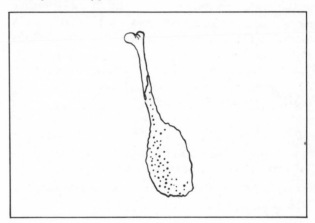

Yarn Drumsticks

Materials:

One-foot length of 1/4" dowel, or a long pencil with eraser

Pencil eraser to use with dowel

Yarn, any color

White glue

Glue the eraser to one end of the dowel, or use the pencil. Wind the yarn over and around the eraser and stick, just as tight as possible. When it gets to the desired size, 1" or so in diameter, cut the yarn. Dab the end, about three inches up, with glue, and hold it in place for a minute. Let it dry thoroughly before using.

The Limber-Jim

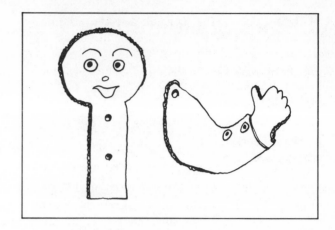

One of the most delightful musical rhythm makers we have ever seen is the little man called "Limber-Jim," also called "Limber-Jack." His counterpart has been found in all corners of the world, from Africa to Russia to the U.S., and is a very ancient toy. This little man is usually on a stick made to hold in the hand, and dances on a flexible board. These dancing men have been found in Europe in much larger sizes. Sometimes they are almost life-size and held on a stick from behind the stage curtain. They are made to dance by holding the stick and moving it up and down. Another one which we have seen goes on the floor on a in Europe in much larger sizes. Sometimes they are almost life-size and held on a stick from behind the stage curtain. They are made to dance by holding the stick and moving it up and down. Another one which we have seen goes on the floor on a bracket. This allows the person dancing him, to keep both hands free for playing an instrument. Whatever size or shape the Limber-Jim, he is fun!

To Make An Easy Limber-Jim

Materials:

Block of wood or piece of board, 2" or 3" wide, 3" or 4" long, and not more than 3/4" thick

A small piece of heavy cardboard or corrugated carton

One popsicle stick

One piece of 1/8" wood paneling cut to about 3" x 21"

A 2' length of 3/8" dowel or straight branch, or wood strip

Tools and Hardware:

Six thumbtacks or upholstery tacks

Eight small cup hooks

One flat-headed woodscrew, at least 1 1/4" long, and thin

Two small nails with good heads

Pliers

Screwdriver

Hammer

Sandpaper

Make a head and arms from cardboard. Use the pattern given or make your own. Cut them out and paint a face and hair, as you like. You can glue yarn or string on the head for hair. One boy I know made a pirate with a patch over his eye!

Tack the head onto the body with thumbtacks, and nail the arms onto the sides, near the shoulder part. Keep the nails out from the body just a bit, so that the arms swing freely.

Cut four sections of the dowel or wood strips, each about 2" long. Screw the cup hooks into both ends of one dowel section and into one end of the other. This is for one leg. Do the same with the other. Put the two remaining cup hooks into the lower part of the body, where the legs will hang.

With the pliers, close the cup hooks on the body and on one end of the dowel with hooks at both ends. Now, hook the open ones into them, and close these with the pliers, so they are all hooked together, legs and body.

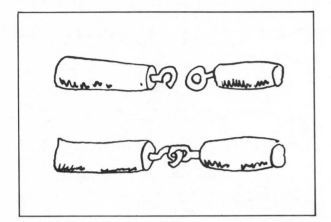

Now Jim needs his feet. Cut the two rounded ends from the popsicle stick, however long you want his feet to be. Sand them slightly, and glue them to the bottom of the lower leg. A tack pushed into the heel of each foot will sound good and tappy when he dances.

To make him complete, put the long wood screw through the body part, just about in the center. Start it in the front and have it come through the back, all the way. Then attach the dowel or branch, which should be sanded first. Press it down on the screw, gently but firmly, and screw it all the way down. If you have a drill handy, a hole can be made in the body and the stick put into the hole.

Suddenly you find your whole little dancing man is together! Sand the dancing board and you're ready to make him do his thing!

How To Dance the Limber-Jim

Sit on a bench or chair with a solid, hard seat. Put the board between you and the chair seat, leaving the longest part of the board extending out to the side. Hold the Limber-Jim stick in your left hand (if you are right handed) and keep his feet *just* touching the other end of the board. Now with the right hand in a loose fist, tap a rhythm on the board. Tap just behind Jim's feet. You can control his dance with the light or heavy way you tap the board, and also make his arms swing around with a very slight movement of the stick back and forth.

Your Limber-Jim will come to life as you make him dance! JOY! Put some good lively music on the phonograph, or sing a song for him yourself, and let him dance to his heart's content. You will grow to love this little man! How about making him a friend called Josie?

Jim A-Long Josie

Traditional
Learned from Lawrence Older

Hey, Jim a-long and a Jim a-long Jo-sie, Hey, Jim a-long and a Jim a-long Joe. Hey, Jim a-long and a Jim a-long Jo-sie, Hey, Jim a-long and a Jim a-long Joe.

Chorus:

E G G G G GA A C̄ E G
Hey, Jim a - long and a Jim a - long Jo - sie,

G G GE E ED D D C̲
Hey, Jim a - long and a Jim a - long Joe.

E G GG G GA AC̄ EG
Hey, Jim a - long and a Jim a - long Josie,

G G GE E ED D D C̲
Hey, Jim a - long and a Jim a - long Joe.

These are the verses sung by Lumberjacks (not limberjacks!) in the Adirondack Mountains:

Verse 1:

E G GG G A C̄ E
Any pret - ty gal who wants a beau,

G G GG E
Just jump in the arms,

E E D D D C̲
Of her Jim a - long Joe.

E G GG G GA A C̄ EG
Hey, Jim a - long and a Jim a - long Josie,

G G GE E ED D D C̲
Hey, Jim a - long and a Jim a - long Joe.

Chorus

Verse 2:
Hitch your oxen to the cart,
And you go to the mill,
And you get a load of bark.
Hey, Jim a-long and a Jim a-long Josie,
Hey Jim a-long and a Jim a-long Joe.

Chorus

Verse 3:
Some is black and some is blacker,
Some is the color of chaw tobacker.
Hey, Jim a-long and a Jim a-long Josie,
Hey, Jim a-long and a Jim a-long Joe.

Chorus

Pattern for the Limber-Jim

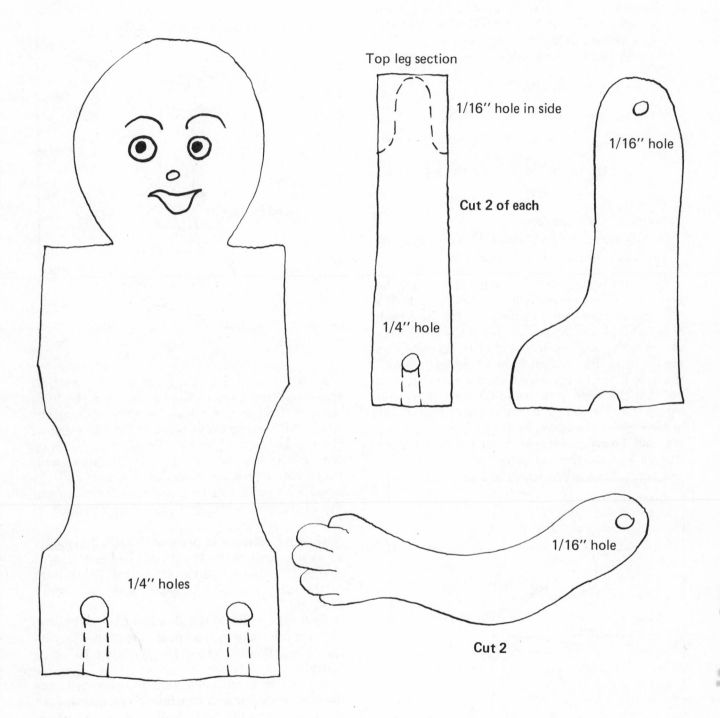

Top leg section

1/16" hole in side

Cut 2 of each

1/16" hole

1/4" hole

1/4" holes

1/16" hole

Cut 2

All Wooden Limber-Jim

Materials:

Clear pine board (or any wood except oak) 3" x 16" and 1/2" thick . . . for body and legs. Pattern on page 37.

Hard board or wall paneling, 1/8" thick—one piece 3" x 4" for arms; the other, 3 1/2" x 21" for a dancing board.

3/8" dowel or straight stick, 15" long

Tools and Hardware:

Coping saw, jig saw or band saw for cutting out body parts

Brace and bit, or electric drill with bits 1/4", 1/16", 3/8"

Hammer

Sandpaper, coarse and fine

Six wire nails 1" long, #18 (small, thin nails with heads)

Two upholstery tacks or thumbtacks

Trace the pattern on the pine board. Cut out the parts with whatever saw you have available. Drill a 3/8" hole in the center of the body for the dowel. Drill two holes with the 1/4" bit in the lower edge of the body, 3/4" up from the edge. As shown on the diagram, draw a straight line from each side of the hole down to the edge, and saw these sections out. Do the same with the lower edge of the top leg section, as shown in the pattern. Round the lower edge of the body, front and back, using the saw and coarse sandpaper. Sand the entire body smooth with the fine sandpaper.

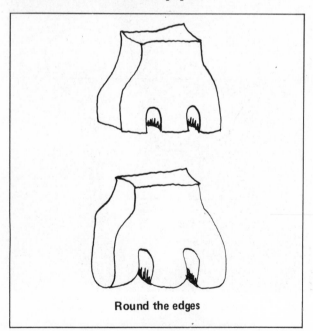

Round the edges

At the top of each of the four leg sections, cut a curve in on each side, as shown in the pattern for the top leg section. Then round the square ends with the saw or sandpaper.

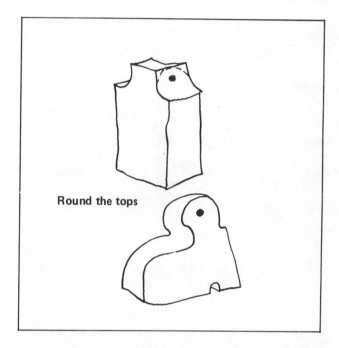

Round the tops

With the 1/6" drill bit, make a hole in each of these four thin parts of the leg, about 5/16" from the top. Drill very carefully, so they don't crack! Also, drill the same size holes in the other end of the top leg section, and in the lower body where the wood has been cut out. Smooth with paper before joining. You can also finish all the wood with paste wax or a commercial finish from the hardware store if you like. Paint the face on first!

Hold leg sections in place with nails. Tap lightly so as not to split the wood. On the lower part of the leg (the "knee" part), the nail will go through to the other side. Tap it gently over, so it won't protrude.

Drill little holes in the shoulder part of the arm, and nail it loosely to the upper part of the body on the side, allowing space for the arms to swing freely.

Put the tacks into the head for eyes. Sand the dancing board, or wall paneling, very smooth. Push the dowel into the body hole, and you are ready to dance! Limber-Jim is rarin' to go! Follow the directions on the Easy Limber-Jim to find out how to dance him.

Melody Instruments

Indian Mouth Bow

The history of the mouth bow should be mentioned, to help you understand its worth as an instrument, although it certainly needs no explanation when someone like Buffy St. Marie uses it for background in a song. It sings its own beautiful song. The mouth bow is believed to be the earliest musical instrument in the world. A series of wall paintings in a grotto at Trois Frères in Ariège, southern France, and estimated to be forty thousand years old, depict a primitive musical bow. Ancient drawings of various types of musical bows have been found all over the world, and to this day, these bows are still being used. The Africans use a bow attached to a gourd for resonance. In the United States, the people in the Appalachians use a mouth bow, much like a jaw harp, but adopted from the American Indian. Several Indian nations are still using instruments in the form of a bow. The Pueblo Indians use a mouth bow for rhythmic patterns to accompany dances. Their mouth bow is made with a string of sinew or fiber, and they use a small wood shaving or bone, ground very thin on one end, for a pick. This bow also has a tuning peg at one end.

Materials:

A tree branch or sapling 3' to 3 1/2' long, about 3/4" wide on one end, and about 1/2" wide on the other. (The type of wood used is quite important. We have found ash, maple, cherry and white birch branches to be the best. The finest mouth bow I ever made was from a black cherry tree in our back yard. It is nine years old and still sounds wonderful!)

One steel guitar string, preferably a B or 2nd string

Guitar pick, light or medium, or cut your own pick from a plastic milk bottle or margarine container.

A wooden tuning peg, or geared banjo peg (optional)

Cut the wood to the desired length. Trim off all leaf ends or twigs to give the branch a clean, smooth look. The small end of the branch should be quite smooth. You may peel off the bark, if you prefer. Cut a slightly angled groove into the branch about one inch from each end, just deep enough to hold the string wrapped around it.

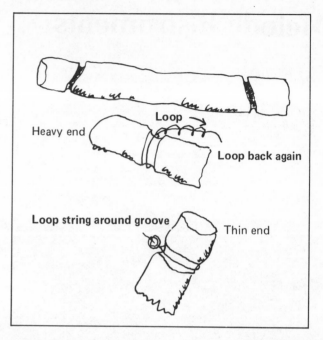

Now the string may be put on. You will find a small metal ring on one end of the guitar string. Run the plain end of the string through this, making a loop which will slip around the thin end of the bow, in the other groove. Holding this end on the floor, with the string in your right hand, and the bow in your left, press the bow down into a curve, making one half to one third of a circle. Now, wind the other end of the string around it several times in the other groove. When you feel it is secure, but still holding the bow so the tension hasn't been released, twist the string down around the open part about seven times, and then back up to the groove. Tuck the rest of the string neatly out of the way, and cut off any extra.

To play the mouth bow, right handed (reverse for the left!): Hold the bow in your left hand, a little more than halfway down, with the string to your right. Place the small end against the right side of your cheek, beside your mouth. (Not in it!) Open your mouth so it will act as an echo chamber. By changing the size of the opening in your mouth, you will be able to vary the tone of the notes. With your right hand, you will hold the pick between the thumb and first finger. Make the pick go back and forth across the string as fast as you can. Begin by doing it very slowly, and then try it at a faster pace! If you have never played a stringed instrument with a pick, give yourself a little time to become familiar with this action. To start with, just plunk down on the string, and when that becomes comfortable, try going back and forth slowly. It will become easier and easier. Actual notes can be made by bending the bow very slightly as you play.

To make the mouth bow tunable so you can play with other people and change keys, drill a hole in the thick end of the branch, and put in a banjo tuning peg. Or use a violin peg, or one you've cut out yourself (how-to directions in the Table of Contents). Drill a hole to fit the peg exactly. Run your string through this instead of tying it around the groove . . . and TUNE UP!

You can have fun decorating the mouth bow, carving designs into it, or tying bright feathers at the bottom. If you carve, be careful not to weaken the wood. I made several for friends with wood-burnings in them, which were very attractive.

Play the mouth bow for an accompaniment to "The Old Soldier," or a song which you already know. You should practice the rhythm on the mouth bow over and over until it is almost automatic. Here is one basic strum to learn for lots of songs (the pick will go in the direction of the arrows):

1 + 2 + 3 + 4 +
/ / / /

Down — Down — Down-Up Down-Up
V   V   V ∧ V ∧
/ / / /

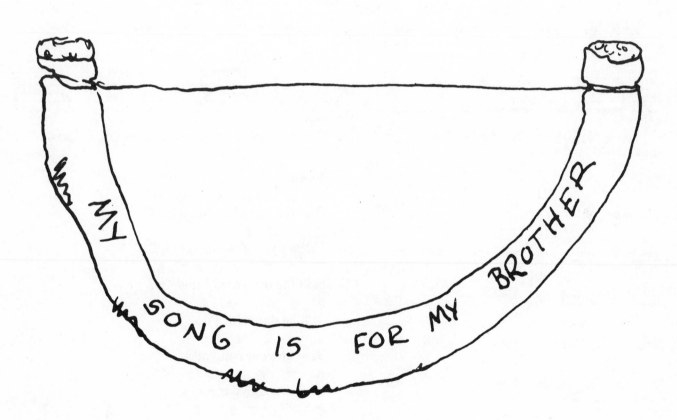

MY SONG IS FOR MY BROTHER

The Old Soldier

Traditional

Oh, there was an old sol-dier and he had a wood-en leg. He had no to-bac-co but to-bac-co he would beg. An-oth-er old sol__ dier as sly as a fox, he al - ways had to - bac - co in his old to - bac - co box.

Verse 1:

				V	∧
V	V	V	∧	Oh	there

was an old sold - ier and he

had a wood - en leg. He

had no to - bac - co but to-

bac - co he could beg. An -

oth - er old sold -ier as

sly as a fox, he

al -ways had to - bac -co in his

old to - bac - co box.

Verse 2:

C̄ C̄ A A A B
Said the one old sold - ier,

C̄ D̄ Ē Ē Ē
"Won't you give me a chew?"

C̄ C̄ Ē Ē Ē D̄
Said the oth - er old sold - ier

C̄ B A A A
"I'll be durned if I do.

A A A B C̄
Save up your pen - nies,

D̄ Ē Ē Ē
And save up your rocks,

C̄ C̄ Ē Ē Ē Ē D̄
And you'll al - ways have to - bac - co,

C̄ B A A A AA
In your old to - bac - co box!"

Verse 3:

Well, the one old soldier
    was feelin' very bad,
He says, "I'll get even, I will by gad!"
He goes to the corner,
Takes a rifle from the peg,
And stabs the other soldier
    with a splinter from his leg!

Plumber's Pipe Cross Flute

Materials:

A 15" length of 5/8" plumber's PVC pipe (plastic). Call a lumberyard which sells plumbing supplies.

One large cork, whittled down to about 7/16" in width to fit into the pipe.

Tools and Hardware:

Two small C clamps, or make a frame to hold the pipe while you work on it. (Nail two strips of wood down to a wide board or the workbench, with the pipe in between so it won't roll.)

Electric drill or brace and bit, with a 5/16" bit

Thread, any color, for decoration

Clamp the PVC pipe to the table with cardboard under the clamp to protect it, or use the holding frame described above. Mark VERY CAREFULLY with a pencil:

3 1/2" from the left end of the pipe
4" from the first pencil dot
1" from the second dot
1" from the third dot
1" from the fourth dot
5/8" from the fifth dot
1 1/4" from the sixth dot
2 1/4" to end

Drill each hole carefully and directly in the center of each pencil mark. If you are afraid of the drill's slipping too far through the pipe into the other side, slip a piece of dowel, smaller than the pipe, into the section you're drilling, and drill away!

Push the whittled cork down into the left end. It goes in 3 1/4", (1/4" from the edge of the first hole).

Not necessary, but very decorative, are the threads for wrapping. Choose any color, and wrap in the areas which will make an attractive design. Put a dot of glue at the beginning and end of each thread to hold it in place.

To Play a Cross Flute

The cross flute takes lots of PATIENCE! Once you have the feel of how to blow across the mouth hole, you will be able to play it happily! It may take a week of practice, but a week is a short time, really, and you will be so glad you stayed with it.

Blow very gently ACROSS, not into the hole at the end with the cork plug. Your gentle breath flowing over the edge of the small hole makes the air inside vibrate. Actually the air is touching the far side of the mouth hole. Put your lower lip next to the hole, and move it ever so slightly away from you, making a "puh" sound until you can hear a flute tone. Once you get the feel of making sounds, then you can work on the fingering.

Here is a chart for fingering the cross flute (black holes mean the finger is covering the hole; open holes show the hole is uncovered):

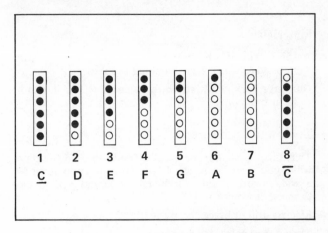

Make up some tunes of your own for practice, and then try some with numbers in this book. Here's one to play, and guess the name of it.

E	D	C̲	D	E	E	E
D	D	D		E	G	G
E	D	C̲	D	E	E	E
D	D			E	D	C̲

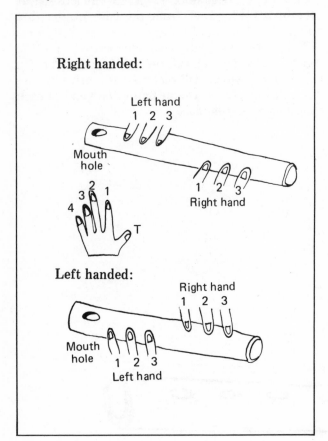

Right handed:

Left hand
1 2 3

Mouth hole

Right hand
1 2 3

3 2 1
4   T

Left handed:

Right hand
1 2 3

Mouth hole

1 2 3
Left hand

Chimes . . . All Kinds

Nail Chimes

Chimes can be very simple with all kinds of varied tones, or they can be carefully tuned so as to produce a clear scale. They may be used for decoration and a lovely sound, or they can be used to play tunes. This is your chance to experiment with different sounds, using various materials.

Materials:

One very small embroidery hoop, or make a hoop from a thin twig or branch, bound together with fine wire

A dozen nails, 6" long or more (they can vary in size)

Carpet thread or thin string

Cord or thin wire to hang the hoop

Cut twelve lengths of carpet thread or string the same size—at least 12"—and tie the nails at the head end to each one. Keeping the strings about the same length, tie the other ends to the hoop. Attach the cord or wire to four sides of the hoop, above the nails, to make a hanger, and bring it up to tie or twist over the center. Hang it anywhere so it moves freely, and the nails can touch each other. Different lengths will make different tones.

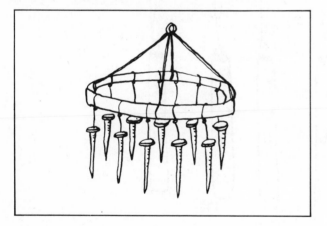

Tin Can Lid Chimes

Materials:

Five tin can lids, various sizes

Hammer, and a nail for a punch

Dowel, or smooth, straight branch, or stick about 20" long

Carpet thread or thin string

Punch holes near the edges of the can lids, one hole in each. Hammer around each hole to make it smooth. Cut five lengths of string or thread, about a foot long, and tie one to each lid. Tie the lids to the dowel or stick, making them various lengths, but so they touch each other as they move. You may want to notch the spot on the stick or dowel where they hang so they will not slide around. It is fun to hang the whole set of chimes in a window. It makes a lovely window wind chime!

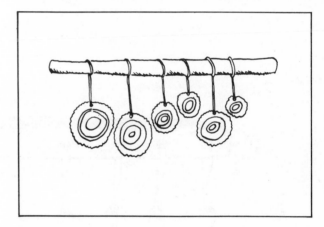

Wood Strip or Dowel Chimes
(You can play tunes on these.)

Materials:

Three 3' lengths of 1/2" dowel, or hardwood strips

Eight small cup hooks, or plain hooks from the hardware store

A 2' long board or stick, to hang the chimes on

String or carpet thread

Tools and Hardware:

Hammer and eight small nails

Saw and pliers

Measure and cut very exactly eight lengths from the dowel: 12", 11 1/2", 11", 10 3/4", 10 1/4", 9 3/4", 9 1/4", and 9". Sand the rough ends *very slightly.* If you sand a lot, it will change the sound.

Screw one cup hook into each dowel at one end.

Tie a 6" string loop onto each cup hook. Hammer the eight nails into the hanging board, about 1 1/2" apart, and hang the chimes from them. You will need to find a convenient place to hang the board so that the chimes hang freely, and you can play them easily.

To tune the wooden chimes, you can change the sound slightly by sanding, or trimming down *very little* if the sound needs to be higher. If it must be lower, cut a very small groove into one side of the wood with a saw.

If you cannot tune the chimes yourself, ask someone with some musical know-how to help you get the scale correct. Actually, if you were very exact with the length of each chime, it should be pretty accurate.

Try a tune on your chimes. Pick something out by ear, or how about trying "The Bear Went Over The Mountain"? Letter the chimes, so you can follow the tune.

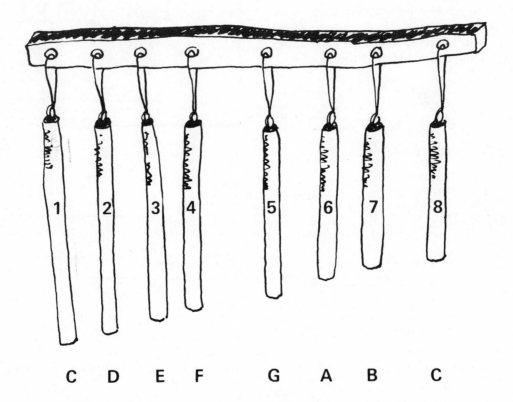

C   D   E   F   G   A   B   C

The Bear Went Over The Mountain

G E E E D E F E			G E E F F E
The bear went o - ver the moun - tain,			And all that he could see,
E D D D C D E C			G G E E E D E F E
The bear went over the moun - tain,			Was the oth - er side of the moun - tain,
C E E E D E F A			E D D D C D E C
The bear went o - ver the moun - tain,			The oth - er side of the moun - tain,
A G F E D C			C E E E D E F - G A
To see what he could see.			The oth - er side of the moun - tain,
E G G A A G			A G - A G F D C
And all that he could see,			Was all that he could see.

Wooden Tuning Pegs

These may be used to replace the metal screw eyes, in any of the instruments, and will probably last much longer.

Materials:

A 1" x 3" piece of hardwood for each peg (unless you want much longer or larger pegs)

Tools and Hardware:

Coping saw or band saw (you will need a small C clamp to hold the wood, if you use a coping saw)

Drill, or brace and bit with a 3/16" bit and a 1/16" bit

Round 3/16" wood file

Pocket knife and sandpaper

Follow the pattern below and cut two pieces out of the wood.

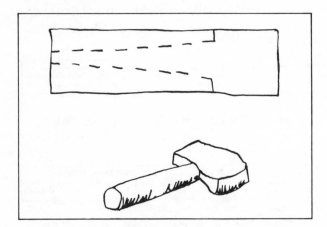

Carve the narrow part down into a round, wider at the top end. Sand it smooth. The lower end should not be less than 3/16" across. Drill a peg hole into the instrument at a slight angle with the 3/16" bit. To make the tapered peg fit into this hole, you will need the round file to taper the hole. When it is a snug fit, put the peg in, using some soap for ease. Mark a dot where the string should go into the peg. Remove it and drill another small string hole with the 1/16" bit. Sand the large end of the tuning peg, replace, and string 'er up!

One Stringed Dulcimer

Materials:

One length of 1" x 2" board about 33" long. Hardwoods are best, but NOT oak. (It's hard to get staples into oak.) Pine and softer woods are adequate.

Tuning peg (three choices!)

1. 3/8" or medium-sized screw eye

2. Banjo geared tuning peg

3. Violin peg, or make your own (see Table of Contents)

One popsicle stick, split lengthwise, sugar stirrer, or small dowel, sanded flat on one side

One 5-string banjo or guitar string (#1 or #2), or very fine wire.

Tools and Hardware:

Small 1/2" nail with head

Hammer

Pocket knife

Coping saw (only if you need to make a groove for the popsicle stick)

Staple gun and staple (3/16")

Drill and small bit (if you make a homemade peg, or use the violin peg—bit must be the same size as the small end of the peg)

Sand the wood very smooth. Follow the diagram for placing the nut and bridge, using either popsicle stick, sugar stirrer, or dowel. Draw lines for the staples, measuring very carefully from the diagram.

Fret Diagram for Dulcimer Neck

You will find it impossible to set staples in with complete accuracy, but try to draw the lines in as near to the specifications as possible.

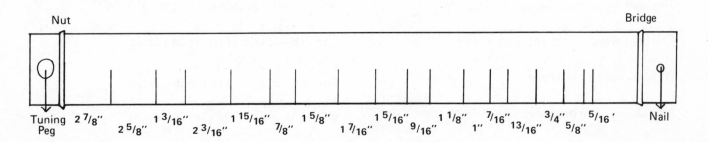

Set in the staples down the whole neck, following the marks carefully. These will be your frets, under the string.

Make grooves with the coping saw or penknife, for the popsicle stick bridge and nut, as shown on the diagram. If using the dowel, just glue the flat side down, and clamp or weight it down with a book or a brick.

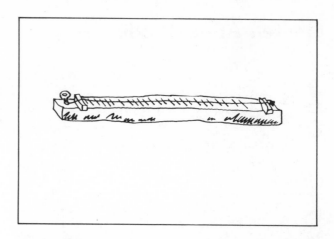

For installing the tuning peg:

1. Screw eye peg. Screw it into the end marked "tuning peg" on the diagram. Put it in only deep enough to hold, so when you wind the string on it, it can be knotted once and tightened around the screw eye.

2. Geared banjo peg. The banjo peg can be set into a hole and drilled to fit, with the part to hold the string on the top. The tuning key will be underneath.

3. Homemade or violin peg. For either of these, drill a hole to fit the peg very snugly. Sand it out where you need the angle to fit well.

Next, hammer the small nail into the opposite end, lining it up with the tuning peg and staple frets. The nail will hold the looped end of the string. The other end of the string goes up to the tuning peg and is wound on. Make a tie in the string, on the screw eye, or run it twice through the other types of peg. Tighten the string until it makes a pleasant sound and is comfortably tight. Now, with the pocket knife, carefully make a notch into the wood bridge and nut, just enough to let the string slip in and keep it in place while playing. Don't make the groove deeper than 1/8".

To play the one-stringed dulcimer, make a small round stick for a "noter." A wooden dowel, garden stake of bamboo, or even a round pencil can be used. You hold this in the left hand, pressing down on the string between the frets. With the right hand, you can strum with a pick, made from a plastic milk bottle or margarine cover. Place the dulcimer on a wooden table, running lengthwise—the tuning peg will be to your left (for right handers). Brush the pick TOWARD you in a steady rhythm, while you press the notes (or finger, if you prefer) between the frets to make your tune. The noter or finger will slide up and down over the frets to change the notes.

Try a cardboard box for a sounding board, or place the one-stringed dulcimer on several different objects to see the variety of sounds you can make.

Below is a diagram to show you the notes on the one-stringed dulcimer. The ending note for most tunes will be the third fret or space.

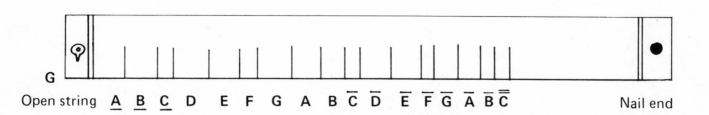

G   Open string A B C D   E F G   A B C D   E F G A B C   Nail end

Go Tell Aunt Rhody

Traditional

Verse 1:

E E D <u>C</u>   <u>C</u>
Go tell Aunt Rho - dy,

D D F   E   D <u>C</u>
Go tell Aunt Rho - o - dy,

G G F   E   <u>C</u>
Go tell Aunt Rho - dy,

<u>C</u> D <u>C</u> D   E <u>C</u>
The old grey goose is dead.

Verse 2:
The one that she's been savin',
The one that she's been savin',
The one that she's been savin',
To make a featherbed.

Verse 3:
She died in the millpond,
She died in the millpond,
She died in the millpond,
A-standin' on her head.

Verse 4:
She only had one feather,
She only had one feather,
She only had one feather,
Right in the middle of her head.

Repeat first verse.

Scarboro Fair
Traditional

This one starts and ends on the *fourth* fret.
3/4 time

```
D  D  A  A  A  E    F   E  D
```
Are you go - ing to Scar - bo - ro Fair?

```
A  C̄  D̄  C̄   A  B  G  A
```
Parsley, sage, rose - ma - ry and thyme.

```
D̄   D̄  C̄  A  A  G  F  E–C
```
Take this word to one who lives there,

```
D  D  A    G F E  D   C̲ D
```
If he would be a true love of mine.

On Top Of Old Smokey
Traditional

3/4 time

```
C  C̲  E  G  C̄    A
```
On top of old Smo - key,

```
A  F  G   A  G
```
All co - vered with snow,

```
C̲ C̲  E  G  G  D
```
I lost my true lov - er,

```
D  E  F  E  D  C̲
```
From a - courtin' too slow.

```
C̲   C̲   E  G C̄ A
```
Now, court - in's a pleasure,

```
A  F   G  A G
```
And part - in's a grief.

```
C̲  C̲ C̲  E   G G   D
```
But a false heart - ed lov - -er,

```
E F   E  D C̲
```
Is worse than a thief.

Kum Ba Ya
Traditional

4/4 time

```
C̲  E  G G   A  A G
```
Kum ba ya, Lord, Kum ba ya.

```
C̲  E  G G   F  E D
```
Kum ba ya, Lord, Kum ba ya.

```
C̲  E  G G   A  G G
```
Kum ba ya, Lord, Kum ba ya.

```
F    E    D  D C̲
```
Oh . . . Lord . . . Kum ba ya.

Sourwood Mountain
Traditional

4/4 time

```
GG  GG  G   A   C̄ C̄  G  E
```
I got a gal who lives in the holler,

```
C̲  E  D   D  D    D E
```
Hi, ho, did - dle dum a day.

```
G  G   G   G A C̄  G  E
```
She won't come and I won't call her,

```
C̲  E  D   D  D    D C̲
```
Hi, ho, did - dle dum a day.

```
Ē   C̄   D̄   D̄ C̄ A   C̄  A
```
Roos - ter's crow - in' on Sour - wood Moun - ta

```
C̲  E  D   D  D    D E
```
Hi, ho, did - dle dum a day.

```
Ē  C̄  C̄ D̄   D̄ C̄  A C̄   A     G
```
So ma - ny pret - ty girls I can't count 'em,

```
C̲  E  D   D  D    D C̲
```
Hi, ho, did - dle dum a day.
```
```

Thumb Harp

This is a fascinating little instrument, fashioned after the African kalimba. Children in Africa carry them around and play tunes, which they improvise or make up. Sometimes they are held inside a very large gourd, so the sound comes back to the person playing it. They believe this makes them feel the music and the sound more deeply.

First make a box, or use a wooden cigar box, any shape. If you can't find scraps of wood around home to make a box, you can get the following from the lumberyard:

3' length of 1" x 1 1/4" lath

1/8" wall paneling—cut two 6 1/2" x 5" pieces

White glue

Several tiny nails

A hammer

Drill with one bit, about 1/4" size

Cut the lath into four pieces: two 6 1/2" lengths, and two 4 1/2" lengths. Make a box frame, setting the shorter sides in between the longer sides. Glue, and then tack with small brads or nails. Take one of the two pieces of wall paneling for the top side, and drill several small holes into the lower half, not too near the edge. Make a design with them. These will be your sound holes.

Glue these two pieces to the frame, and wrap with heavy elastic bands or inner tube bands to hold it all together until the glue is set. Sand and finish the wood. Now you're ready to make the playing part.

Materials:

Six metal rake tines (don't use the family rake!). Cut these into 2 3/4" lengths, and sand all the paint off. (A small round metal rod, hammered flat, also works well.)

6" length of half round

6" length of lath ripped down to make 1/4" x 3/4" strip.

Two 6" pieces cut from a wire coat hanger

Tools and Hardware:

Hammer

Metal file

Wire cutters

White glue

Heavy rubber bands, or inner tube cut into bands

Four round-headed wood screws 5/8" #5

File the rake tines, rounding one end for playing, and the other end straight and smooth. Also, file down the ends of the coat hanger wires.

Make a groove in the 6 1/2" length of wood, just deep enough to keep the wire from rolling off.

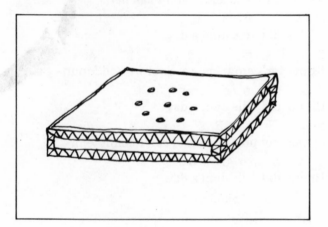

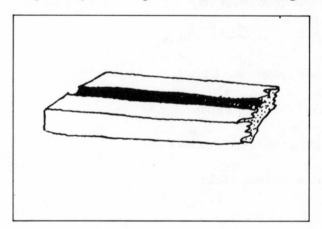

Hammer four holes into the flat side of the half round to help start the screws. Space the holes evenly and directly down the center. Also, make four starting holes in the piece with the wire, just enough to allow the screws to get a hold in the wood.

Now put the rake tines in between the two sections of wood, and resting over the wire. Place the tines with the rounded ends to the wire side, and screw the half round down into the under-piece with the wire.

When this unit is together, glue it at an angle to the top of the box, opposite the sound holes. Hold it in place with the rubber bands, and let it sit overnight.

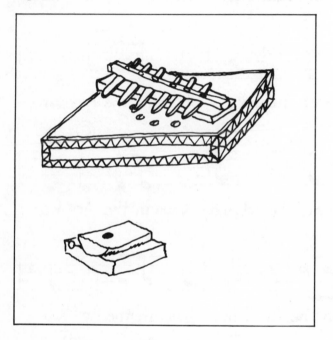

The rake tines are your "keys," and to tune them you must pull them into a pattern. The left keys are longer for the lower notes, and they get shorter and shorter to the right for the higher notes (like the diagram). Now you are ready to match it to the piano diagram or have someone help you tune it.

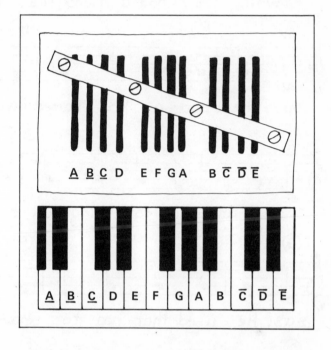

PRESTO! It's ready to play! Pick something out by ear, or make up your own melodies like the young people in Africa do. If you end your song on the low end, third key (C or 1), it will sound best. How about trying "Down in the Arkin"?

Down In The Arkin

Traditional

Well,_ I had a friend, his name was Jack, down in the Ar-kan-sas. He had a hog named Raz-or-back, way down in the Ar-kan-sas. Fun-ni-est thing you ev-er heard, down in the Ar-kan-sas. He used that hog to shave his beard, way down in the Ar-kan-sas.

Chorus:

Down in the Ar-kin, down in the Ar-kin, down in the Ar-kan-sas. The pret-ti-est gal I ev-er saw was down in the Ar-kan-sas.

Verse 1:

C̲ DE EE C̲ F F F
Well, I had a friend his name was Jack,

E G G E D
Down in the Ar - kan - sas.

G G G G F F F
He had a hog named Raz - or - back,

F E EE DD C̲
Way down in the Ar - kan - sas.

E E GG G A F F
Fun - ni - est thing you ev - er heard,

E G G E D
Down in the Ar - kan - sas.

G G G E F F A
He used that hog to shave his beard,

F E EE DD C̲
Way down in the Ar - kan - sas.

Chorus:

G GG G E C̄ C̄ C̄ A
Down in the Arkin, down in the Arkin,

G G G C̄ E D
Down in the Ar - kan - sas.

D E E C̄ A AF F
The prettiest gal I ever saw,

F E EE D D C̲
Was down in the Ar - kan - sas.

Verse 2:
Well, I had a mule named Simon Slick,
Down in the Arkansas.
He'd turn his back and then he'd kick,
Down in the Arkansas.
So when you meet him with a load,
Down in the Arkansas,
You'd better give him all the road,
Down in the Arkansas.

Bread Board Zither (and Simple Psaltry)

Materials:

One bread board or solid piece of hardwood. (I used cherry. The size, at least 10" x 15".)

A 2' length of screen molding from the lumberyard, or 3/8" half round. Make a groove to hold the wire.

Two straight bottom sections of coat hanger wire, one 10" long, the other cut into three 3" pieces.

Guitar or 5-string banjo strings from the music store You need three of each: #4, #3, #2, and #1.

Tools and Hardware:

Jig saw or coping saw (only if you want to scroll the top)

Brace and bit, or drill with bits, 1/2" and 3/8"

Screwdriver

Twelve screw eyes (5/8" x 1 3/8" is a good size)

Twelve round-headed brass wood screws, 1/2" #4, or small size.

If you have a jig saw or coping saw, you can design and cut out a fancy scroll for the top of your zither. If not, there's no problem, and don't bother with it. Perhaps you could wood-burn or paint a design in the unused part at the top.

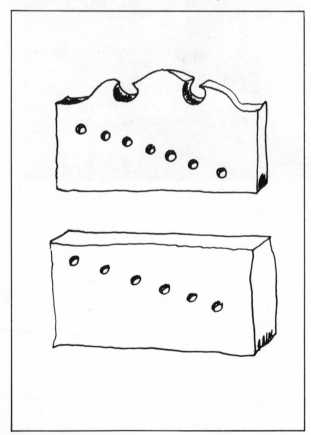

Drill several sound holes, using both size bits to make an attractive pattern. Set them up about 7 1/2" from the lower edge. When you drill, place an old board underneath, so the bit can run into it and not leave split or fuzzy edges on the back.

Cut a 10" length from the screen molding to fit along the lower edge of the board. Cut three 3" lengths for the top. Sand the ends and glue the molding in place after marking the board with a pencil. The lower edges of each piece of molding should be:

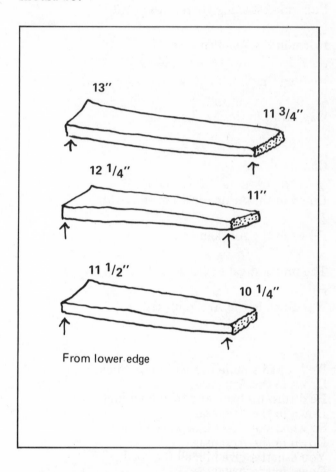

From lower edge

The small molding strips should be glued down about 1/4" in from each side: they will be very close to each other as they go into place.

Put heavy weights like books or bricks down on the molding, top and bottom, until the glue is set. Allow at least half an hour for this.

While you're waiting, why not finish the wood? Sand with fine sandpaper and put on a good paste wax or commercial finish from the hardware store.

Fit the coat hanger wires into the grooves of the molding pieces, and put dabs of glue on to hold them in place, if you wish. These wires give the strings a solid bar to rest on so they won't cut into the wood.

Now put in the screw eye tuning pegs. Mark off with a pencil four dots, 3/8" in from each end of the 3" moldings, 3/4" apart from each other. Set these dots about 1/4" behind the molding strips. Angle the screw eyes slightly as you turn them into the wood. This gives more support for the strings. Turn the screw eyes in only a little way.

Screw in the brass screws at the bottom of the board into the pencil dots, marked off evenly. Leave a little space with each screw for the string to slip over and hold.

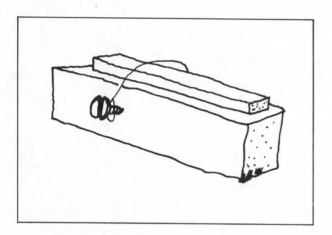

Now you're ready to string it up! The strings go on in the same order over each strip; #4 to the left, then #3, #2 and #1.

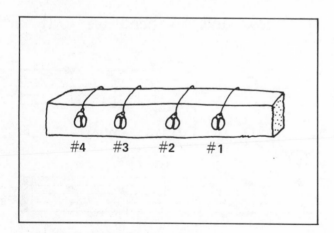

#4   #3   #2   #1

After putting the loop end over the brass screw at the bottom, take the other end and loop it twice or tie it around the eye in the screw eye. Allow about two inches slack on the string, because the screw eye cannot go too far into the wood, and the less string to wind up, the better. Wind the string around lower part of the screw eye and tighten it *slowly!* Do the same with each string. When it's all strung up (hope you're not all strung out!) tune it to a piano, or ask someone around to help you tune it.

This zither is strung up to play chords, or groups of notes while you sing along, as you would with a guitar or banjo. Lots of books have songs with chords written over the words, which you can use with the Bread Board Zither.

You can tune to chords on the piano, if you have one, using the diagrams below. Tune the groups of strings to the chords C, F and G.

	C	F	G
Notes:	c e g c	f a c f	g b d g

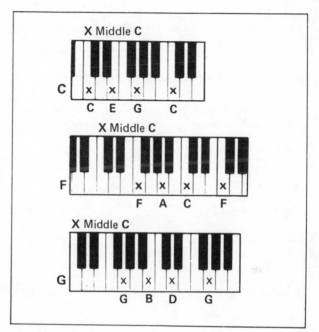

Hold the zither in your left arm, facing away from you, so the right hand can finger the strings easily. Walk the fingers over the strings for each chord, while you sing the melody. Play on the strings which go with the chord written above the words, while you sing the tune. You can use the note letters for the one-stringed dulcimer. It would be fun to have a friend play along with you!

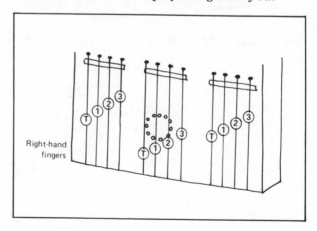

Simple Gifts
(Shaker Hymn)

'Tis the gift to be sim-ple, 'tis the gift to be free, 'tis the

gift to come down where we ought to be; and when we find our-selves in the

place just right, t'will be in the val-ley of love and de-light.

When true sim-pli-ci-ty is gained, to bow and to bend we will

not be a-shamed. To turn, to turn_ will_

be our de-light, and by turn-ing, turn-ing we come 'round right.

G G̲ C̲ C D E   C̲
'Tis the gift to be sim - ple,

E F F G G F E
'Tis the gift to be free,

D C̲ D D D   C̲
'Tis the gift to come down,

D   E D   B G̲
Where we ought to be.

G̲ C̲ B C̲ D   E-C̲
And when we find our - selves,

E F G   G-F E
In the place just right,

D C̲ D D D D E
It will be in the val - ley,

D C̲ C̲ C̲
Of love and delight.

G E D E F E D C̲
When true sim - pli - ci - ty is gained,

D E E F G F E D D D E D
To bow and to bend we will not be ashamed.

G̲ C̲   D E C̲ E-F G G F E
To turn, to turn will be our delight,

D C̲ D D E   E
And by turn - ing, turn - ing,

D C̲ C̲   C̲
We come 'round right.

Simple Psaltry or Psimple Saltry

Follow the directions for making a Bread Board Zither, but the psaltry will have a different string arrangement, so you can play melody on it.

Instead of three 3" strips at the top part, you can place one long 9" strip of molding at an angle in the same area. The high part at the left side should be placed 10 1/4" from the bottom edge. Glue it down and weight or clamp for at least a half hour.

About 1/4" behind the top molding, make a mark 3/8" from each side. Then mark twelve dots in a row, each 3/4" apart. These will mark the places where your tuning pegs or screw eyes will go in. Mark the same spacing arrangement at the lower end, and put the brass wood screws in for the string pegs. String it up and tune it to a C scale on the piano, or have someone help you.

This lovely instrument will be a delight, and you can pick out lots of tunes by ear. Try making up some songs of your own!

Devil's Dream

Your own one-man band! A little like the washboard but with more musical possibilities. They used to sell something like this in the old Sears catalog.

Materials:

(These will cost a little more than some of the others, but it will be well worth it!)

One rake handle

2' length of lath or lattice from the lumberyard

A popsicle stick

5" or 6" pot lid (take of knob), or use real cymbal

From the music store:

8" or 10" tambourine with jingles (you can also use a child's tambourine from the Five and Ten . . . much cheaper).

5-string banjo bridge

#4 5-string banjo or guitar string with loop end

One violin tuning peg, 3" long

Metal kazoo

Cowbell

Make your own clack box and drumstick (see Table of Contents). You can also add bicycle horns and any other noise gadgets!

Tools and Hardware:

Small saw

Hammer

Sandpaper

Brace and bit, or electric drill with 3/8" bit

Small 1/4" round-headed wood screw

4 1/2" round-headed wood screws

Drill a 3/8" hole four inches down from the top of the rake handle in the exact center of the pole for the violin peg to fit into. Sand the peg down to fit the hole. It should be snug, but not too tight. Rub soap on the peg so it turns easily. Push the peg gently into the hole, and keep sanding and soaping until it feels just right.

The tambourine has a row of jingles around it. Remove the jingles from two opposite slots by pulling out the nails. Cut a 13" strip of lattice and sand the ends. Hold the back rim of the tambourine against the rake handle, on the side where the tuning peg holds the string. Slip the lattice strip over the back of the rake handle and into the two slots in each side of the tambourine. Screw two of the 1/2" screws through the lattice, into the rake handle to hold them together.

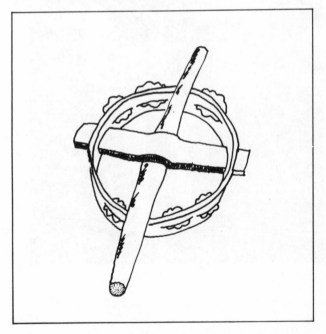

Put the tiny 1/4" screw into the tambourine at the lower end, directly over the rake handle. This will hold the string, so screw it only partway in. Cut the popsicle stick to match the width of the pole. Make a shallow groove with a saw across the pole, 1 5/8" beneath the peg hole on the front side. Glue the popsicle stick into this groove. This will be a nut for the string to run over. If it is too high and wobbley, trim it down with sandpaper.

Make a very small notch in the top edge for the string.

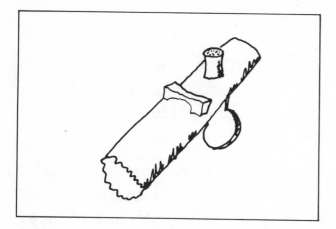

Make a light pencil mark on the face of the tambourine for the bridge: 4" up from the lower end of the 10" tambourine, and 2" up from the lower edge of the 8" tambourine. Put the string on, looping it over the little screw, running it over the banjo bridge. The string will hold the bridge in place. Wind the string twice through the little hole in the tuning peg, leaving several inches over, so you won't have so much to wind. Tighten the string JUST enough so it sounds musical! Be sure the bridge is centered under it.

Hammer the nail through the center hole of the pot lid cymbal. Be sure the nail is a little smaller than the hole, so the cymbal is free to vibrate when you tap it. Drill more small holes in the neck if you want to fasten the clack box and cowbell, or anything else. Use wire or string to fasten them.

Screw the small strip of leftover lattice a little below the peg hole on the back of the neck. Use two screws. Wire or tape the kazoo to this, to that it's at an angle that allows you to hum into it easily.

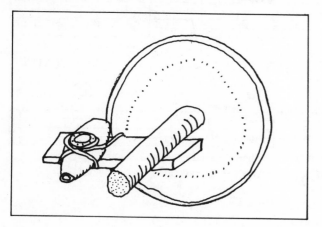

To play the kazoo: The small paper diaphragm inside the top part vibrates with the air stream. In case you haven't tried playing a kazoo before, you DON'T blow! HUM any tune you wish into the wide end. It comes out sounding like a frog with a sore throat, but it makes a fun bluesy, ragtimey sound, so good in a jugband, or your own one-man band!

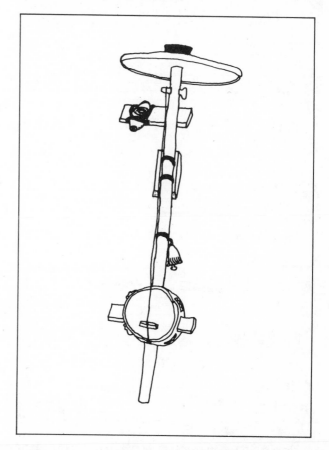

You can also learn to play melody on the string of the Devil's Dream. Hold one finger of your left hand down on the string with the rest of your hand behind the neck, the way you would hold a guitar. Now pick the string with your right hand. If you slide the left hand up and down the string, the notes will change from higher to lower. Try picking out a simple tune. Tie a drumstick to your wrist or to a cord around your waist, and use it on the drumhead, cowbell and clack box for rhythm. Now you are armed with all you need to sound like Mac Namara's Band itself!

One Bottle Of Pop

(A Round)

Verse 1:

C̄ C̄ C̄ C̄ C̄ C̄ C̄ C̄ C̄ C̄
One bot - tle of pop, two bot - tles of pop,

G G G G G C̄ C̄ C̄ C̄ C̄
Three bot - tles of pop, four bot - tles of pop,

C̄ C̄ C̄ C̄ C̄ C̄ C̄ C̄ C̄ C̄
Five bot - tles of pop, six bot - tles of pop,

G G G G C̄
Seven bot - tles of pop . . .POP!

Verse 2:

C̲ C̲ D E F G E E
Don't throw your junk in my back yard,

F D D E C̲ C̲
My back yard, my back yard,

C̲ C̲ D E F G E E
Don't throw your junk in my back yard,

F D D C̲
My back yard's full!

Verse 3:

C̲ D E F G A G
Fish and chips and vin - e - gar, . . .

G̲ A G G A G
Vin - e - gar . . . vin - e - gar,

C̲ D E F G A G
Fish and chips and vin - e - gar . . .

G A G C̲
Vin - e - gar . . .POP!

Dallas Cline

For Children Who Love To Sing And For Adults Who Love To Sing With Them

Songs for a New Generation
by Evelyn Challis
This series (*Jumping, Laughing and Resting; Fun Songs, Rounds and Harmony; Love, Work and Hope*) provides the material together with a few simple instructions to help parents and teachers involve children in the joy of expressing themselves through song.

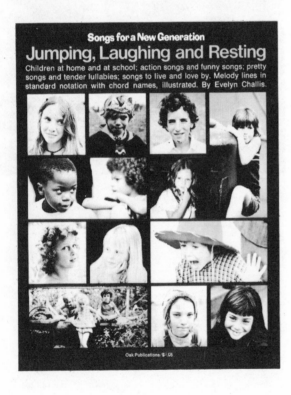

Jumping, Laughing and Resting
For the littlest ones (ages 3 to 10) this book includes a wide variety of *action* songs for fingers, thumbs, hands and feet; notes by Ms. Challis on interesting ways to present the songs; and ideas on how to deal with so-called "non-singers." Standard music notation and chord names.
$4.95

Fun Songs, Rounds and Harmony
This is a beautiful collection of songs which includes rounds from the simplest to the most complex. These are tunes that Ms. Challis has found to work extremely well, even with children who have never before sung in harmony. Contains African, Spanish, Yiddish, Hebrew and German songs, with English translations of the verses. Joyously illustrated, with music in standard notation and chord names. For children 8-14.
$4.95

Love, Work and Hope
This book contains soft and tender love songs and philosophical songs about the way things are and could be. It's for children 12 on up and is beautifully put together and easy to use.
$4.95

These books are available at your local music store or directly from:
Oak Publications
33 West 60th Street, New York, NY 10023
Please add 50¢ for postage and handling.
Write for FREE catalog.